ALSO BY TIP O'NEILL

Man of the House

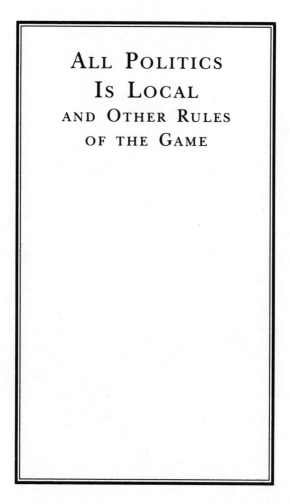

ALL POLITICS
IS LOCAL
AND OTHER RULES
OF THE GAME

ALL POLITICS
IS LOCAL

AND OTHER RULES
OF THE GAME

★

Speaker Tip O'Neill

with Gary Hymel

T I M E S 𝕿 B O O K S

R A N D O M   H O U S E

Copyright © 1994 by Thomas P. O'Neill and Gary Hymel

All rights reserved under International and Pan-American
Copyright Conventions. Published in the United States by
Times Books, a division of Random House, Inc., New York, and
simultaneously in Canada by Random House of Canada Limited,
Toronto.

Library of Congress Cataloging-in-Publication Data

O'Neill, Tip.
All politics is local and other rules of the game / Thomas
O'Neill with Gary Hymel.—1st ed.
p.   cm.
ISBN 0-8129-2297-2
1. O'Neill, Tip. 2. United States—Politics and
government—1945–1989. I. Hymel, Gary. II. Title.
E840.8.O54A3   1994
328.73′092—dc20   93-29988

Manufactured in the United States of America
24689753   23456789   98765432
First Edition
Book design by Jo Anne Metsch

To the friends Millie and I have met through life

≡ Contents ≡

≡ Introduction ≡

This book is a *primer* on politics, or at least politics as practiced in my sixty years of experience. I state a principle then illustrate it in a story that I hope gives the rule some meaning.

Storytelling is the easy part. Sometimes I had to think hard what the principle was. For me politics always was about values combined with instincts. Put those together and you get a rule.

Storytelling comes easy to me because I used anecdotes to keep an audience entertained—and make a point. It's a sad commentary on today's politics that storytelling is disappearing. Campaigning today is all sound bites on TV and trying to put a fresh spin on your message.

When I started out, a candidate had to walk the district and appear at night rallies whose only audience was the one within earshot. I guess I could hone a good story by telling it over and over without worrying that someone there had already heard it.

If I were running today, I probably would have to

use all the modern techniques of political campaigning: hiring a political consultant, polling extensively and making ads targeted to TV audiences.

In my early days, the government was so small, the national deficit was only about $4 billion a year. Today it is in the hundreds of billions, and counting. Budgets are figured in trillions. The government is in so much of our lives that politics has had to take on a different meaning. But there are some things about politics that never change: giving your word and keeping it is still the bedrock. Loyalty to your party, faithfulness to your constituents and keeping your head are some of the others. "All politics is local" is probably the lesson most associated with me. Actually, my father first told it to me and it helped me greatly along the line. I can't tell you how many people come up to me and repeat it, giving me the credit. My story about never forgetting to ask people for their vote has also come back to me. Once a fellow approached me and said that principle had gotten him elected attorney general of New Jersey. "I read your autobiography and never forgot to ask everyone I met to vote for me," he said. "You elected me."

Having a sense of humor is another good principle in political life, and that gets us back to storytelling. I once worried I was wearing out my stories and asked the comedian Danny Thomas for some new ones. He had just heard me tell some of my old standards.

"Tip," he said, "you don't need new stories, all you need is new audiences."

So let's get started.

Oh, one more thing. There are a few of these stories

you may have read or heard from me before, but as far as I'm concerned they never get stale. They are still true, and part of me. They are too important to leave out of this book.

★

▦ All Politics Is Local ▦

I lost the first race I ever ran, for the Cambridge City Council, by 160 votes because I took my own neighborhood for granted.

My father took me aside after the election and told me, "All politics is local. Don't forget it."

I never did. Every time I ran I did a survey of my area, to see how it had changed. I remember when we counted 25,000 workers in the candy factories and how the number dwindled to nothing over the years. I remember counting 8,000 students at MIT and learning there were 12,000 employees there. Harvard had 8,000 students, too, but only 5,000 staff. With eighteen colleges and universities in my district, we had 200,000 students, and that meant education had to be a priority with me.

Winston Churchill got beat because he neglected his electoral district while he was leading Great Britain in World War II. Sam Rayburn almost got beat when he was Speaker of the House of Representatives.

George Bush let his great triumph in the Gulf War

distract him from domestic politics. Look what it got him.

A politician learns that if a constituent calls about a problem, even if it's a streetlight out, you don't tell them to call City Hall. You call City Hall.

Members of the House learn this quicker than anyone else because they only have a two-year term. They learn that if you don't pay attention to the voters, you soon will find yourself right back there with them.

I tell them to pay attention to their own backyard and take care of their folks. Get home often and report to their constituents. Keep them informed and you will find they will like and respect you and allow you to be a "national" Congressman and vote for things that are good for the country but may not have a direct impact on your district. Of course, it's better if you can say you voted a certain way because it was "good for the economy of the area," but you don't always have that reason.

This is what I mean when I say, "All politics is local."

★

No. 1
Campaigning

≡ 1 ≡

Location, Location, Location

Real estate people will tell you these are the three most important factors in evaluating a piece of property.

They don't have a monopoly on that principle.

One time in 1960 we were hosting the candidate for vice president of the United States, Lyndon Johnson, in Boston, and Jack Kennedy called me, worried we would not be able to draw a crowd and would embarrass the ticket in his hometown. The rally was scheduled for Mechanics Hall and we had worked for days with labor unions calling people to come. We even had the curtain drawn across half the hall to shrink the size of the potential space to fill. That afternoon, hours before the evening rally, we had LBJ out in Copley Square and someone pointed out that the insurance company workers were about to get off work and start heading to the subway—right past us. I wanted LBJ to get their attention.

So we wheeled in a flatbed truck, and then I got a better idea. I walked over to a mounted policeman, talked him off his horse and got LBJ up on it. Well, that created a sensation. Hundreds of people swarmed around him and the horse. It got on the evening news and everybody saw it. We got a big crowd that night. We even had to take that curtain down to fit everyone in.

Be in the right place at the right time and then make the best of it.

★

2

Four Essential Ingredients
of a Campaign

I always tell a crowd gathered at a fund-raiser for a candidate that there are four elements to any campaign—and you'd better pay close attention to all four.

They are the candidate, the issues, the organization and the money.

Over the years, those ingredients have not changed—only the money has increased a whole lot.

In my first race for city council, I spent $35. I lost but got noticed. I ran only 160 votes behind the eighth and last person elected, and the *Boston American* wrote that I was a "figure to watch in the future."

Next, I ran for state representative, increased my budget more than tenfold, to $400, and won. The most I ever spent was $200,000, in 1984, when a Texas millionaire financed a candidate against me—but despite all this spending he only did one percentage point better than my opponent in the previous election.

Today, I see a candidate spend a million dollars to

get elected to the Congress of the United States. To me, that's ridiculous. Having to raise so much money has distorted the process and undermined it.

But here's the sometimes forgotten trick about money: despite these big amounts needed today, people still like to be asked to participate. They even like to be asked for money, and even $5 or $10 can make a difference. But they want to make a contribution if the candidate, the issues or the organization earn their support.

★

☰ 3 ☰

Never Look at How Much Each Contributor Gives

This is a tough one. Most people don't believe me when I say I wouldn't look, but you're better off if you don't. You and your friends and supporters work hard raising money from among your other friends and supporters. They give in varying degrees, based on what they can afford. The natural temptation is to take a look at who gave what. And your staff will say, "Look at what this SOB gave. And all that help you gave him for years."

Don't look. It will tempt you to help only those who gave, and that's wrong.

Of course, you don't have to let anyone know you don't check. I told one of my contributors I never look and he told me, "I wish I'd known that before. I wouldn't have given you so much in the past."

★

≡ 4 ≡

People Like to Be Asked

Asking is the most important part of a campaign. It's amazing to me how many politicians forget that.

On election day of my very first campaign, one of my neighbors, Mrs. Elizabeth O'Brien, stopped me and told me, "Tom, I'm going to vote for you tomorrow even though you didn't ask me to."

This shocked me, to be perfectly truthful. "Why, Mrs. O'Brien," I said, "I've lived across the street from you for eighteen years. I cut your grass in the summer, I shovel your walk in the winter. I haul out your ashes. I didn't think I had to ask for your vote."

"Tom," she replied, "let me tell you something: People like to be asked."

Every election day as Millie and I left for the polls, I'd say, "Honey, I'd like to ask for your vote."

"Tom," she'd reply, "I'll give you every consideration."

★

≡ 5 ≡

Don't Create an Opponent for Yourself

Back in 1984, I got a call from Bill Barnstead, who had run against me three times as a Republican.

"Tip, do you want me to run against you or don't you want me to run against you?" he said.

"What?" I said, astonished.

"Do you want me to run against me or not?" he repeated.

"Bill, I don't care if you run against me or not." I had clobbered him every time he ran. "Why are you asking me?"

"Well," he said, "the only reason I ran against you before was because back in seventy-four at the Chamber of Commerce of Belmont, Arlington and Watertown you said you believed that Republicans ought to have a full slate to run against every Democrat. You said something about the democratic process, and that an opponent forces an incumbent to report to the people.

"I took you seriously and that's the only reason I ran."

Boy, did I learn something there. I could have saved myself a lot of time and money if I had just kept my big mouth shut.

★

≡ 6 ≡

How to Handle a Token Opponent

Of course, all politicians have to recognize when they are in a serious fight, but all of us draw token opponents along the line. You can't allow them to sap your strength. How you handle them is as important as handling the big ones.

Back in 1964, a fellow came into the office in Boston and told my secretary, Dorothy Kelley, that he was running against me. "I hereby challenge Mr. O'Neill to a debate," he announced.

Dorothy was taken aback because no one had run against me in ten years. This was something new.

She replied, "I think you must be in the wrong office because no one is opposing Mr. O'Neill."

"Well, I am," he said.

"No," she insisted, "I think you must mean someone else because if someone were running against Mr. O'Neill, someone certainly would have mentioned it."

Well, it devastated the poor guy. He slunk out of the office and never filed.

I can't remember his name.

★

≡ 7 ≡

How to Turn a $5,000 Contribution into $50,000

Many years ago, in the fifties, when I was in the Congress of the United States, I was appointed by Sam Rayburn to a special committee to go to Ireland for the dedication of the statue of John Barry. Now, if you went to public school you probably believed that John Paul Jones is the father of the American Navy, but if you went to a parochial school like I did, you'd know that John Barry was the father of the American Navy.

I went over with my wife, Millie. It was my first trip to Ireland. We drove down around Cork City, where my father's people came from. We stopped, of course, and kissed the Blarney Stone, we rang the bells of Shandon and we went around the marketplace where the women are so picturesque in their dress.

During one tour, the driver suddenly stopped the car and said, "That's our local hospital."

"What's so unusual about that?" I said. "Every community has a hospital."

"It's very interesting," he said. Then he explained how Henry Ford had helped build the hospital.

Ford had been visiting Cork, the home of his parents, when a group of men greeted him. They welcomed him to his parents' birthplace and asked him to make a donation in their memory for a new hospital.

Ford sat down and very graciously wrote out a check for $5,000. They thanked him.

The next day, the Cork newspaper announced, incorrectly, that Ford had made a donation for $50,000. The group of men returned to Ford's hotel room to apologize for the mistake and promised that the newspaper would make a correction.

Instead, Ford asked for the men to return his check. He wrote them a new check for $50,000, which he handed to them with only one request. "Over the portals of this hospital," Ford said, "I want an inscription I have in mind."

To this day, the inscription reads: I CAME AMONG YOU AND YOU TOOK ME IN.

★

≡ 8 ≡

Persistence Pays—
but Don't Fool Yourself

One of the great storytellers around the statehouse in Boston was Patrick "Sonny" McDonough. Jim Curley had belittled him one time when he was running for Mayor with the line "Imagine someone named 'Sonny' wanting to be Mayor." But Sonny persisted. Senator Leverett Saltonstall, with another snide remark, had made fun of him for trying to get the state's insurance business for his agency: "Sonny wants to get the fire insurance on the Bunker Hill Monument!" But Sonny persisted.

Sonny used to tell the story of Mike Sheehan running for office in South Boston. He went up to each house with a pad of paper in his hand marked "yes" and "probable." He would tell each person who answered his knock, "I'm a candidate for the statehouse and I'd like your vote." If they answered, he would make a note under the appropriate column. The "no's" he didn't bother writing down.

He goes up to this one house and the lady of the house answers and he goes through his routine. She replied, "Are you the Michael Sheehan who is the son of old Mike Sheehan?" He allowed that he was.

"Well, that old reprobate. He's a bum so you must be too."

He put her down as a "probable."

★

≡ 9 ≡

Be Generous with Your Greetings but Don't Overdo It

In every Congress there are some great storytellers, but Congressman Bill Hungate of Missouri is an all-around entertainer. He tells stories, plays the piano and writes ditties, always in the spirit of fun and friendship.

Once during a campaign swing through Bill's district, we had a small political party, asking for votes and raising a few dollars. Bill said, "These people will love you. They'll like your accent and your smile, so just shake hands." Well, that was easy, politics is the same the world over. Bill would shake hands and turn and say, "Meet my friend, Tip O'Neill." Then I'd shake hands and give with the small talk. Bill didn't miss a single person. He's the greatest politician I ever saw with a handshake.

Finally, as we were about to leave, Bill reached out and shook a fellow's hand and said, "Have I shaken your hand before?" The fellow said, "This is the third time tonight."

We all had a good laugh.

★

≣ 10 ≣

To Raise Campaign Money, You've Got to Make the Calls

My leader in the Massachusetts statehouse lost the race for governor because he didn't have enough funds. He was at odds with the state Democratic committee and they wouldn't share the master contributors list with him. We all got together and used the Yellow Pages to call every doctor, lawyer and small business man we could. We raised about $125,000, but it wasn't enough.

Old Ben Franklin had some good advice, like most of his wisdom as good today as when he uttered it. "First," said Franklin, "call upon all those you know will give something; next apply to those you are uncertain whether they will give or not; and finally those who you are sure will give nothing, for in some of these you may be mistaken."

★

≡ 11 ≡

No Contribution Is Too Small

Bob O'Hare was doing advance work for Jack Kennedy and they sent him to Maine. One night he got a call: "Is this Bob O'Hare who is working for Jack Kennedy?"

Told it was, the caller continued, "Well, I'm a doctor up here and I'm a Catholic and I'd like to contribute but I don't want anyone to know about it. So I'll walk to the corner drugstore and leave it in an envelope on the mailbox."

Bob agreed and retrieved the envelope. He opened it. It was only ten dollars—in a presidential campaign. But Bob took it. Maybe the guy had some relatives in Massachusetts where the votes would do some good.

★

≡ 12 ≡

In a Campaign, Get Volunteers Involved

When we opened a campaign headquarters, we would immediately recruit as many volunteers as we could.

We would get someone to stop by for a half hour or so—a young mother, a teenager, a shift worker—to address envelopes or make calls. We'd get others to look up addresses and phone numbers. Then they would go home and tell their friends and neighbors how they were "working in Tip O'Neill's campaign."

The truth is, sometimes we'd have to throw the envelopes away because we couldn't afford to mail them, but we had a friend for life.

Today, with so much of the campaigning done on TV, we tend to forget this human factor.

★

≡ 13 ≡

How to Become a Senator

When I was in the hospital with cancer, I was very depressed because I had to have a colostomy and wear a bag the rest of my life. Millie was sitting with me and noticed how down I was. She looked at the mailbags in the room (I had gotten about 30,000 letters) and she said, "Pull one out and read it."

I opened one from a Tom Findley, who had been Harry Truman's first secretary in the Senate. He told me how Truman had been a judge but he was really more like a county commissioner. He couldn't get by on the judge's salary so he asked the political boss of Kansas City, Tom Pendergast, for a job as a county assessor because it paid more.

"Pendergast told Harry he wasn't smart enough to be a county assessor, so, he said, he was going to send him to the Senate."

★

≡ 14 ≡

A Vote's a Vote

Jimmy Duncan, Jr., a fine congressman from Tennessee—even though he is a Republican—whose father served the district before him, tells the story of how he got a put-down and a vote at the same time.

It seems he got a call from a seventy-eight-year-old retired schoolteacher named Hazel West from Scott County, Tennessee, a small rural county on the Kentucky line in the Cumberland Mountains.

He said, "Hazel was a very frank and plainspoken woman and when my father asked for her vote she said no, adding, 'You're too good a man to put you in Washington.' My father tried to persuade her by pointing out that her two sisters were voting for him but she answered, 'But they don't take this as seriously as I do and they don't think as much of you as I do.' "

Jimmy continued, "I asked her if she had ever voted

for my father over the years. She said she hadn't. 'Did you vote for me?' I asked. 'Yes,' she said. 'You're not nearly as good a man as your father was.' "

★

No. 2
Speaking Out

1

Never Get Introduced to the Crowd at Sports Events

This is a temptation for a lot of politicians and it's hard to pass up.

When Paul Dever was governor of Massachusetts, he presented the winner's cup at the Governor's Handicap at Suffolk Downs racetrack. He was booed loudly and the newspaper the next day ran the headline GOVERNOR BOOED AT THE RACES. I believe it started his downfall and he lost the next election.

Once I went to a Marvin Hagler championship fight in Worcester with a couple of old friends. Well, one of them knew the promoter and he was excited about introducing me from the ring. "Don't do it," I begged him. "I just came to see the fight."

No sooner had I settled into my seat than I hear this booming voice coming over the microphone. "Ladies and gentlemen, we are privileged tonight to have with us one of the great men of Massachusetts, the Honorable Tip O'Neill, Speaker of the House of—" He didn't even get to finish, the boos and catcalls were so loud. The microphone was useless. And I was in my own state. I laughed it off, thanking my lucky stars I wasn't in the middle of a campaign this time.

People go to sports events to enjoy the action. They feel intruded upon if some outsider imposes on what they paid good money for.

My well-intentioned friends had to learn that one the hard way.

★

2

Never Forget Your Spouse

This is one I always tell the new freshman class coming into Congress. It's an easy one to forget because your spouse usually has been at your side during the campaign, and, to be perfectly truthful, you get into a routine, share the same ups and downs, and sometimes forget to be grateful.

I was reminded of this through a story I heard about how a congressman, "Pete" Peterson of Florida, made a speech at his fund-raiser in Washington. At the end, he added, "Now I'd like you all to meet the biggest contributor to my campaign." He paused. "My wife." The place burst into applause and everyone present had been reminded of a good lesson.

Spouses leave their relatives, friends, a job perhaps, and move lock, stock and barrel to a strange city trying to keep things running without missing a step.

Others stay back in the district and make do with a weekend relationship. Whatever, their support is a crucial asset.

My Millie certainly did it for me. When I was off to Washington helping run the country, she was back home running the family. When I was at my low point in politics, she was giving me a hug and telling me to go out and do my job. When I was in the spotlight taking the applause, she was in the background cheering me on. I love her for it.

★

3

Know Your Audience

Once I was invited to deliver a St. Patrick's Day speech before the Friendly Sons of St. Patrick in Wilkes-Barre, Pennsylvania. A piece of cake, or so I thought. I figured those Irishmen would arrive early for the dinner, have a few pops (that's drinks to you outlanders) and by speech-making time would be receptive to anything I said as long as I kept it short and humorous. A few stories and I would get out of there.

Unfortunately, it didn't work out that way. As I was in my hotel room dressing, one of my aides came in out of breath. He had just found out no drinking was allowed before the dinner—only afterwards. Now suddenly my audience had changed. I had to give a serious speech. Luckily, my staff had copied some pages from a book *Famous Irishmen in America*. All through the preliminaries and during the dinner, I was flipping through these pages and underlining passages.

When I got up to speak before this thoroughly sober crowd, I was ready. They applauded afterwards and complimented me on my thoroughness. Ha!

★

4

To Be a Successful Public Speaker, Memorize Some Poetry

One day Jim Curley heard me make a speech and told me I was lousy. He invited me to go around to his home.

"I'm going to give you ten poems and essays to memorize," he said. "Never again will you be in the position you were in the other night, because you can always recite one of these to fit the moment. Believe me, people love it when you give them a quote, especially when you do it off the top of your head. They might not remember anything else from your speech, but they'll remember that."

Here's Jim Curley's list:

1. Polonius' famous speech to his son, Laertes (from Shakespeare's *Hamlet*)
2. "The Deserted Village" by Oliver Goldsmith (long poem)
3. "It Can Be Done," by Edgar A. Guest (poem)
4. "Abou Ben Adhem," by Leigh Hunt (poem)

5. "Around the Corner," by Charles Hanson Towne (poem)
6. "If," by Rudyard Kipling (poem)
7. "Friendship," by Ralph Waldo Emerson (essay)
8. "Psalm of Life," by Henry Wadsworth Longfellow (poem)
9. "The Man in the Glass," author unknown (poem)
10. "Rules of the Road," by John Boyle O'Reilly (poem)

★

5

Never Attack an Opponent's Family

I heard this first from Harry Truman. I met him with
a group of us freshmen when I first came to Congress
in 1953 and the conversation turned to Mamie Eisenhower. Truman said that he had no use for Ike.

"But leave his family alone," the President continued, his voice rising. "If I ever hear that one of you
attacked the wife or a family member of the President
of the United States, I'll personally go into your district and campaign against you." Truman may have
been a lame duck, but he was still fighting the good
fight.

I've always followed Truman's advice, and the one
time I slipped up there was hell to pay. It happened
thirty years later, when I was Speaker, Reagan was
President, and James Reston from *The New York Times*
came in to interview me.

Early in our conversation, he asked me about Nancy
Reagan. I made a facetious remark to the effect that
when the Reagans were through—which I hoped

would be in 1984—they could return to California, where Nancy could be queen of Beverly Hills.

The next day, when the quote appeared in Reston's column, I felt just terrible. I sent a letter of apology to Mrs. Reagan, but by then the damage had been done. To this day I feel bad about it.

What's worse are the mean cartoons and jokes about the children of Presidents. Amy Carter and Chelsea Clinton, for instance, are not fair game. It's hard enough for them to try to grow up normally in the spotlight. They should be off-limits to the press.

★

≡ 6 ≡

Beware of Handouts

I committed to vote for a bill that would guarantee that 50 percent of any U.S. foreign aid had to go in American ships. It was good for my district and good for the Seafarers' International Union, who asked me to help.

The day of the vote, as I was about to enter the House chamber, one of the SIU lobbyists handed me a speech and asked me to make it in support of the bill. I took it, sat down and began listening to Congressman Jimmy Roosevelt speaking on the bill. At the same time I started looking over the speech I had been given. It looked familiar. It was. It was the same speech Jimmy was giving, word for word.

I learned a lesson that day: Make sure your speech is original before you deliver it.

★

≡ 7 ≡

Know Your Lines

When you are making a speech, you must know what you are saying and say it like you know it.

I learned my lesson in the senior class play at St. John's High School.

Everyone in the class had to have a part in the play and they gave me one line to say. I was the butler, and when the star asked, "Is my chariot ready?" I was to say, "It is." That's all: "It is." I rehearsed it with them every day and then I would run out to baseball practice.

You guessed it. On the only performance of the play, the lead asked, "Is my chariot ready?" I blurted out, "IS IT?"

★

8

Keep Your Speeches Short

Lincoln's Gettysburg Address was 271 words. President Clinton's inaugural address of fourteen minutes was his best speech. John Kennedy's legendary inaugural speech was only a few minutes. One of the great orators of our time, Bishop Fulton Sheen, taught me to keep my speeches short. The bishop was one of our early television stars, along with Milton Berle, Ed Sullivan and the Honeymooners.

I had met Bishop Sheen at my daughter Rosemary's graduation from Dumbarton University when he was the commencement speaker. His niece was graduating too. At a party the night before, I asked him how long his address was going to be. (I had been to graduations before.) "I used to speak for an hour," he replied. "But one time as I was just getting started, a gust of wind blew away my text and I had to wing it on my own. People told me it was the greatest speech I ever gave. I had spoken for eighteen minutes. It taught me that's what the attention span is, about eighteen minutes."

"How do you know when to stop?" I asked. He replied, "I set my watch at sixteen minutes and after it goes off, I wind up in two."

I don't know the source of that wind gust, but I got the message too. I tell a couple of stories to get the audience's attention, give 'em eighteen minutes of serious stuff, then close it off with another story.

Keep your speeches short and the audience will remember what you had to say.

★

≡ 9 ≡

Acknowledge a Good Crowd

Ed Muskie, who should have been President, was a guy I knew from the beginning of his career. I'll never forget when he was elected governor of Maine as a young man in 1953. He was being paraded around the country as the New Beginning for the Democrats, a knight in shining armor on a white horse.

He came down for a big rally for our candidate for governor in Massachusetts, Bob Murphy, got a big standing ovation and replied, "I'm reminded of the old dairy farmer who got up one cold December morning. It was eight below zero. He put on his woollies, his mackinaw, his heavy gloves and his fur cap and went to milk the cows.

"He put the pail under old Bossy, took off the gloves and commenced to milking. Old Bossy turned to look at him and said, 'Thank you for the warm hand.' "

★

≡ 10 ≡

Everyone Has a Hero

Millie is always telling me I talk too much, and I'll admit that a successful politician should be a good listener. But there are times when you have to take charge of a conversation and become the catalyst.

I was at dinner with a group of big-business leaders, their wives and the expert pollster Peter Hart, and the conversation started dragging.

Peter spoke up to get things going. "Who have you ever met that when you shook their hand, your own palm started sweating?"

Well, that kicked off a lively round of talk as each person told his or her story about Ronald Reagan, Hubert Humphrey, on it went.

Now, I have had the privilege of meeting leaders from nations around the world along the line, but when it got to me, my answer was easy.

"Ted Williams," I said. "It was on his seventy-third birthday, and it was the first time I had met him."

Now, you are probably shocked that I had never

met him before because you know what a baseball fan I am, especially of the Red Sox.

But as many times as I had seen Ted in Fenway Park since he broke into the major leagues in 1939, as many times as I had said publicly that he is the greatest hitter I had ever seen, I had never met him.

When I finally did meet him at the birthday, I mentioned this to him and he said, "People tell me all the time, you must know Tip O'Neill." And here's the reason we had never met: "Tip," he said, "I wish you were a Republican."

"Ted, I wish you were a Democrat," I retorted. Politics aside, I still think he was the greatest hitter I ever saw.

★

≡ 11 ≡

Don't Give Speeches That Are Pure Bunk

The word *bunk* is a common American slang word. It comes from politics. In 1820 there was a senator, Felix Walker, who used to engage in what was obviously useless talk. He was from Buncombe County, North Carolina, and those speeches for back home took on a shortened nickname: *bunk.*

When I was presiding over the House of Representatives of the Congress of the United States, I would see these members approach a microphone with a dark suit, a blue shirt and a red tie. I knew they were going to make a "bunk" speech for home consumption only.

Now, I am proud that I was the Speaker who first allowed the cameras in to record the sessions—ahead of the Senate by six years, I might add. And Brian Lamb, whose idea C-SPAN was, does a great job expanding democracy by showing the House in action to over 60 million families.

But we worried that members would abuse the privilege of television by playing to the cameras. They have.

I don't think these speeches help at home. The people see them for what they are and they can even do damage.

The best speech makers are responsible and treat their audiences with respect.

★

45

≡ 12 ≡

A Speech Remembered
Is a Speech with One Memorable Sentence

Who can forget Jack Kennedy's "Ask not what your country can do for you—ask what you can do for your country."

And FDR's "We have nothing to fear but fear itself."

Or Lincoln's "With malice toward none and charity to all."

President Clinton may well have made his contribution with "There's nothing that's wrong with America that what's right with America can't fix."

One of my favorite stories is about a fellow who ran for state auditor in Massachusetts, Tom Buckley. The party leaders had put him on the ballot to fill an empty spot on the ticket. No one knew much about him.

Well, he got the nomination and then had second thoughts. He worried that he would lose his job with the W.P.A. if he won the election. So he went underground. No one could find him. WHERE'S TOM BUCK-LEY? the headlines ran.

Finally the Democratic Party held its convention in Springfield and Buckley showed up. He appeared on the platform, seated next to House Speaker John McCormack. McCormack noticed how nervous he was because of all the publicity and his lack of political sense.

McCormack told him, "Just get up and tell them you're an auditor, not an orator. And sit down."

He got up, said, "I'm an auditor, not an orator," and sat down.

He won, of course.

★

≡ 13 ≡

When Making a Speech, Watch Who's Ahead of You on the Program

When Hale Boggs was the majority leader of the House, I was the whip. He invited me down to Baton Rouge, Louisiana, to address the statewide AFL-CIO convention. I figured this was an easy one for me and I'd get a chance to go to New Orleans, eat some good food and walk around Jackson Square, which I do every time I'm there.

Well, my dear friend Hubert Humphrey preceded me on the program and I went to the hall at the appointed time, 11:00 A.M., to be ready to go on as he finished. He had started at 10:30. Ha! At 11:00, Hubert was just getting warmed up. He went for at least an hour and a half and he had those union members on their feet cheering most of the time. Hubert finally finished to a thunderous applause with 4,000 delegates clapping in unison. Some Girl Scouts presented Hubert with a bouquet of roses. He walked off the stage, and, it being lunchtime, the delegates left, too, to get something to eat.

Vic Bussie, the great Louisiana labor leader, quickly

introduced me before leaving with Humphrey for lunch at the governor's mansion.

I delivered my ringing oratory before about forty people.

When I caught up with Hubert at the mansion, he apologized for running into my time, but who could stay mad with Hubert Humphrey?

★

≣ 14 ≣

Get by the Second Election and You Have It Made

Nobody worked any harder in an election campaign than I always did. You find your volunteers and staff people do the same—follow the leader. I remember best of all my 1954 campaign for the Congress of the United States. I was running for reelection, running on my record, how I had voted, how my office had served the district, were they doers, were they able to get things done, were they friendly, all things that help the person running for reelection.

There is an old saying, "Get by the second and you have it made." I really worked hard on my second campaign, and when it was over, I said to Millie, wife and fellow campaigner, "I rang ten thousand doorbells, shook twenty thousand hands, walked to four hundred factories, kissed thousands of babies and I can't remember how many women I told they were beautiful.

"I did every kind of campaigning I know of and made two hundred speeches besides."

Millie, always ready to bring me back down to reality, observed, "It's not that you gave two hundred speeches. You gave the same speech two hundred times."

★

"I'll ever think of campaigning." I have to smile every now and then at senators bellowing about "$300 breakfasts." When a Senate page costs one dollar I have never seen one turn in an expense account, including postage.

≡ **15** ≡

If Possible, Speak off the Cuff

Nothing is quite as boring as having to listen to some politician read a speech. More often than not, a speaker will read from a text if there are a lot of statistics involved. This makes it even more tedious.

When we put television in the House of Representatives, we had to put the cameras in the gallery, and since they are pointed down to the House floor, members who read speeches get only the tops of their heads on TV. It's worse if they're bald. The reflection is blinding.

It's much more effective to speak off the cuff, even though it takes more time to prepare what you're going to say.

Once a particular senator read a speech to a lunch group and succeeded in boring everyone. Afterwards a feisty old lady came up to him and said, "How do you expect us to remember your speech when you can't remember it yourself?"

Another time I got into an argument at a dinner

with some big businessman who took exception to my opinion of Ronald Reagan.

"Reagan is great," he said. "He can give a speech without a note. I saw him do it at the State of the Union."

I had a hard time convincing him Reagan used a TelePrompTer, just like all the Presidents do. They read the speech off two glass plates in front of the House rostrum. The audience can't see it but I could, from the Speaker's chair.

That was one of Ronald Reagan's secrets. He could make people believe in his magic tricks.

★

≡ 16 ≡

Don't Indulge Yourself

Most politicians deliver eulogies and testimonials one of two ways. They talk about their relationship with the dearly departed or honoree, and then talk about themselves. Or, they skip the first part and start talking about themselves right away.

The temptation is great to tell about yourself, but no one wants to hear it. Stick to the subject of the gathering and everyone will appreciate it.

★

No. 3
Serving Your
Constituents

≡ 1 ≡

If You Know You're Right,
You Can't Go Wrong

In my first term in the Massachusetts legislature, in the Joe McCarthy era, I voted against a loyalty oath the American Legion was pushing on our teachers. The oath itself seemed harmless, but requiring it at all seemed to cast doubt on a teacher's patriotism. I said to myself, "Why have it if you trust them?"

I was one of two Democratic representatives who voted to repeal it. I just couldn't bring myself to vote for a bill that would question the loyalty of the good nuns who had taught me or my sister Mary, who was a schoolteacher. People said I'd never get reelected, I was done for. The heat was put on me in the next election. The Legion ran full-page ads against me and uniformed Legionnaires campaigned against me at the polls. Hysteria had set in.

I countered with a campaign of explaining my vote to my constituents. Of course, I had worked hard for my people when they needed me. When I needed them, they came to help.

The whole experience had the effect of freeing me

and conferring on me an independence that I carried through a lifetime in politics.

Sticking by my conviction gained their respect—more than their concern for the issue itself.

★

2

Take Care of Your Own

Once I got Jack Kennedy to agree to attend the dinner of the New England division of the Catholic Youth Organization. My old Boston College classmate Father John "Speed" Carroll had asked me.

A few days later, the President himself called Speed. "I'll be happy to do it," he said, "but I want to be in and out. No meetings. Just take me to where I'm supposed to be, give me five minutes to freshen up, and then bring me out to meet the young people."

When the President arrived at the hotel, Speed was there to greet him. "I understand your wishes," he said. "But we have some bishops who are hoping to meet with you, and a group of nuns in the next room."

Kennedy didn't lose a beat. "The nuns I'll see," he said. "But not the bishops. They all vote Republican."

★

≡ 3 ≡

You Can Switch a Position, but Do It Quickly and Openly

Often, one of the members of the House would come by to say that although he had promised the people at home he would vote a certain way, he had changed his mind and wanted to get out of that commitment. What should he do?

"Tell them the truth," I would reply. "Come clean about it, and do it quickly. Issue a statement saying you were convinced by one set of arguments, but now that you've had a chance to hear the other side, you believe your earlier position was mistaken."

I would describe my own reversal on the Vietnam War, and how I patiently explained my new position to the people in my district, some of whom were convinced I was a traitor.

There is a big difference between waffling on a position and honestly changing your mind. Make sure the people know the difference.

Once Sam Rayburn changed a position. "I'd rather be right than consistent!" he declared.

• • •

Another story about switching happened to me in the fifties.

Jack Kennedy had been beaten by Estes Kefauver for the Democratic nomination for vice president, and old Wayne Aspinall, the chairman of the House Interior Committee, had told him why. Aspinall said it was because Kennedy and his supporters were weak in the farm states, never helping on farm legislation.

Jack called the Massachusetts delegation together and asked us to change our vote record and support the farm bill next time it came up. House Speaker John McCormack gave us a great line to explain to our voters why we city pols were supporting agricultural legislation. "As goes the economy of the farm, so goes the economy of America," he said.

I started voting for farm bills and always used that quote. I never once got hurt politically.

Another time, back in the fifties, there was a big effort to send U.S. wheat to Poland. Now in those days communism was in its prime and some saw this as helping out those no-good Commies. I had a solid record of opposing anything that even appeared like something they would want.

Cardinal Spellman of New York City was a leader of the anti-Reds, but he sent down a retired general to see the Catholic House members to urge us to vote for the bill because nearly everyone in Poland was a practicing Catholic. The rationale was, we were helping feed hungry people, not helping a political regime.

I voted for the controversial bill and as I was heading home for Christmas I rode along with a Republican member from New Hampshire. "I'd hate to be you going home for Christmas having voted for that Commie bill," he told me.

Well, it turned out he got beat in the next election and I won.

That one didn't hurt me either.

★

≡ 4 ≡

Beware of Factions

As a politician, you should join a lot of organizations, but going to meetings can get you in trouble.

I know this sounds harsh, but I've seen so many well-intentioned clubs fall apart when they break into factions. So I say politicians should join organizations—the Knights of Columbus, the Elks, the Kiwanians, the Masons—but remember, you don't have to go to all the meetings.

What happens is, controversy develops and the minute you pick a side, you alienate the other side. You can't win. It reminds me of kids who start a club just so they can leave someone out.

One of the biggest fights I ever saw was over who would lead the Charitable Irish, the premier organization in Boston. The contest for chairman developed into a full-blown campaign with lunches and slogans. After it was over, I know people who didn't speak to one another the rest of their lives.

But it taught me a valuable lesson.

★

≡ 5 ≡

In Politics,
No Chore Is Too Small

The tendency in politics today is toward mass appeal, mass mailings, and mass media. But if you don't do the little things, none of this "mass" business is going to work.

We got to talking one day to the fellow who drives us when we are in Florida. He is a very interesting person, having come to this country after the Hungarian Revolution in 1956. He became an American citizen and married an Irish-American who used to write me periodically. Once she mentioned that she was a Democrat, but her husband was a Republican. I couldn't wait to ask him why.

"It's simple," he said. "When I got my citizenship, the senator from Florida, Ed Gurney, a Republican, wrote me a letter congratulating me. I've got it framed on the wall. I cast my first vote for him and I've never failed to vote Republican."

So a routine letter made a difference.

I used to send letters of condolence to widows in my district. I got their names from the funeral notices.

One called me. "Did you know my husband?" she asked sharply.

"No," I said.

"Then why did you write me?"

"Well," I said, "I noticed your husband was in his seventies. I figured you must be too, and maybe you needed help with a Social Security problem."

She hesitated.

Then she thanked me.

★

≡ 6 ≡

Be Grateful for Your Office

Jimmie Burke, the great congressman from Boston who for twenty years worked as hard as any member I served with, had a standard response to other members who complained to him about the long hours and hard work of a politician: "It sure beats heavy lifting."

"I'm not concerned about the hours I work," he would say, "because I always think of what I would be doing if I weren't elected!"

★

≡ 7 ≡

Always Send Them Something

Jimmie Burke was the champion at mailing to his constituents.

One of his practices was to mail every loose piece of material he could lay his hands on to his constituents. "A leaflet a week" was his motto. He used to say that 30 percent of the people never get a piece of mail. (That was in the days before junk mail. On second thought, maybe he started it.)

People used to say, "I love Jimmie Burke, he sends me a letter every week." Asked what the letter was, some would say, "I don't know, I never read it, but he's thinking of me."

Sometimes they'd answer. Once he sent an infant-care book to a woman and she wrote back, "I don't know of any baby in the house—but thanks anyhow."

★

≡ 8 ≡

Show Me Courage and I'll Show You a Following

Harry Truman is looking bigger and bigger every day. Historians rank him with the greatest of the Presidents. People wonder if he knew what he was doing when he dropped the atomic bomb, but he stopped World War II and saved thousands of American lives. His Marshall Plan is legendary. He stood up to the Communists in Korea.

Truman's standing was at rock bottom in 1947. But he came back with a great campaign in '48 and showed what a stand-up, courageous guy he was. Still, the memories of those days when he was despised lingered.

During World War II a lot of industrialists went into the government as dollar-a-year men to make sure the production line rolled so we could win the war.

Truman used to tell about one such mogul, obviously a Republican, as most of them were. This particular chieftain found himself honored at a dinner after he had completed his government service.

"What do you think of Harry Truman?" was the first question from a dinner guest.

"I can't possibly tell you," said the honoree. "If I told you what I thought of that little guy, it would positively shock you."

They tried a couple more times and the industrialist would not respond to the group.

After everyone had gone home, a tough Republican got him aside, whispering, "Now we're all alone. What do you really think of Harry Truman?"

"All right," said the industrialist, "I like the little son of a bitch."

★

9

Getting Elected Doesn't Mean They Love You Forever

Leadership brings with it the people who love to put you on a pedestal so they can throw brickbats and mud at you. The idea of a honeymoon is a myth. Governor Pat Brown of California, father of Governor Jerry, knew the joys of victory and the humiliation of defeat.

When Ronald Reagan defeated Brown for governor, Pat wrote him a letter stating, "There is a message in *War and Peace* that every new governor with a big majority should have tacked on his office wall. In it young Count Rostov, after weeks as the toast of elegant farewell parties, gallops off on his first cavalry charge and then finds real bullets snapping at his ears.

" 'Why, they're shooting at me,' he says, 'me, whom everybody loves.' "

★

≡ 10 ≡

For Every Critic There May Also Be an Admirer

Congressman Charlie Weltner of Georgia liked to tell about a letter he received from a constituent berating him for his voting record, his personality and just about everything under the Georgia sun. The writer promised to devote all his time during the remainder of Charlie's term to defeating him. The letter writer then signed his name, and to the left at the bottom were his and his secretary's initials, as is the custom.

Except at the bottom was the following line: "I have to type this stuff, but I don't have to believe it. I think you're great!" The secretary's initials followed.

★

≡ 11 ≡

A Life of Public Service Shouldn't Make You Rich

When I was Speaker of the Massachusetts House, I earned $9,000 a year. My insurance business brought in another $25,000. What I would do was scan the newspapers in Boston, Cambridge and Somerville for the marriage notices. I'd call up the newlyweds and sell them a policy for ten to twelve dollars a year. I was hoping as they got successful they'd buy more and take some insurance out on their business, too.

In 1971 I was making $40,000 as a congressman and still getting about $7,000 from my insurance business. Of course, I was neglecting it and not adding to it.

When I got in the leadership as whip in 1972, Common Cause noted I had the insurance business and said I should drop it because it was a potential conflict of interest. I did.

I often wondered how successful I would have been if I'd stayed in business. I think I would have made a lot of money. I certainly didn't in politics.

But I wouldn't have had it any other way.

★

≡ 12 ≡

Never Forget
Whence You Came

You campaign hard, listening to all the cheers and taking all the compliments. Then you win and everybody tells you what a great person you are. Then off you go to Washington to dine with Presidents and meet with moguls of business. People recognize you on the street.

It's an easy prescription for excess pride, and good politicians know to be wary of it.

It reminds me of a story about Jack Kennedy. He used to have regular meetings of neighborhood leaders, just to find out what people were thinking.

Billy Sutton, his first secretary, said that at one such meeting Kennedy noticed Eddie Ford, a pal of mine, was absent. "Where's Eddie?" he asked.

Patsy McDuff spoke up: "Eddie's in the hospital. Trouble with his *prosphate.*"

"That's *prostate,*" Kennedy corrected.

Patsy said, "There he goes with that Harvard accent again."

The lesson is: *You* grow but the folks back home may not grow along with you.

★

No. 4
Making Things
Happen

≡ 1 ≡

When Pursuing Votes, Know the Territory

One of the great advantages I had in preparing to run for leadership positions in the Congress of the United States was being chairman of the Democratic Congressional Campaign Committee, which is involved in raising and disbursing funds to elect Democratic congressmen. I had to learn about every congressional district in America, the ethnic, economic and party characteristics of each and the strength of our candidate in each.

In fact, that job helped me so much I became the only person to hold all four jobs in the leadership: chairman of the campaign committee, whip, leader and Speaker.

In the campaign committee I would go out to a district I knew little about and learn a lot. I remember going out for Congressman Phil Burton and learning to appreciate how urban his San Francisco district was. The same was true for Congressman Dick Durbin in Springfield, Illinois, a farming district. And Congressman Bill Hungate of Hannibal, Missouri, a small-town district.

I learned a valuable trick on these trips. When I arrived, I would try to do something that was unique to the district. In San Francisco, it was visiting the beautiful Golden Gate Park Phil had practically built; in Springfield, it was visiting Lincoln's home; and in Hannibal, it was whitewashing Tom Sawyer's fence. Then I would mention these things in my speech. It would soften the audience facing this stranger from the East.

On these trips, I learned what made these members tick and how secure they were, so when I asked them to support a Democratic Party position, I knew how far I could ask them to go. I could handle them.

★

2

Take Care of One Problem
and You'll Often Take Care of Another

When I was Speaker of the House in Massachusetts, Dick Furbush was president of the Massachusetts senate and he used to tell a great story.

It was about a legislator who had been away for a month and had finally gotten home and was catching up on all the local newspapers. His son came in and asked his dad to go outside and play catch. No, the father said, he had to read the papers. Five minutes later the kid was back, pestering his dad.

"Look," the father said, "I want you to do something for me." And with that he took a map of the world, which happened to be in one of the papers, tore it in half, then quarters, then eights and finally into sixteenths.

"Now take this out in the kitchen and put it back together," he instructed.

The kid was back in two minutes with the map assembled correctly.

"My, I'm impressed," said the dad. "There are a

hundred twenty countries in the world and you know them all."

"Well, Dad," said the lad, "there was a boy's picture on the other side of the map and I just fitted it together."

The moral of the story is: Put the youngster together right and the world will take care of itself.

★

≡ 3 ≡

Go with the Pros—
and Train Some New Ones

The best advice I can give a new member of Congress is to hire professional help. There is nothing so valuable as a staffer who can steer you around the Hill, knows how the House functions, and is familiar with the committee system and the important players.

I had a reputation on the Hill for hiring excellent staffers. At the start of the Clinton Administration, one of my former staffers got a job offer to work in the White House. "I don't know Tip O'Neill," the caller said, "but I know he was known to hire smart people." (I guess they figured I needed the help.)

Congressmen have an obligation to youngsters too, and care should go into picking the most junior staffers, even the interns.

I had a practice of hiring about a dozen interns on a three-month basis. I would meet with them, assign them a current topic and ask them to write a paper for me on a given subject.

One of these papers was on sickle-cell anemia, a disease that has a high incidence among blacks. The paper intrigued me, so the next time I saw Dan Flood, the chairman of the right appropriations subcommittee, I asked him about it.

No, he said there was no federal program for it and he had never even heard of the disease.

So I sought out John Conyers, who was head of the Black Caucus, and suggested they get on it.

The result is, today there is over $40 million available for research and a national system of centers to fight the disease.

Good staff can make a difference.

★

≡ 4 ≡

Stay Away from Labels

Nobody likes to be labeled or pigeonholed. It's insulting and it's often a form of bigotry.

Once some author characterized me as a "typical Irish politician." Boy, did that burn me up. I called him up and demanded to know what he intended to imply by that phrase.

"Do you mean a card-playing, whiskey-drinking, cigar-smoking politician?" I asked him.

He apologized.

The truth is, I enjoy all those things. I love to play poker and gin rummy, within my means, of course. Over the years, those games have kept me out of a lot of trouble other fellows have gotten into in the bachelor scene in Washington.

As for whiskey, I never drank before five o'clock, I never drank alone. And I never drank if I had a problem. People say they never have seen me affected by it. I guess this is a place where my weight helps me. To be perfectly truthful, I don't even enjoy the smell of whiskey.

I do enjoy a good cigar, and the doctor told me it's okay to smoke. "It's the last of your vices," he said.

But all that still doesn't make me a "typical Irish politician."

Got that?

★

5

You Can't Win Without the Votes

Whether it's President Clinton trying to get a bill passed or the Speaker settling a fight between two committee chairmen, the essential ingredient of politics is compromise. I love to say that "the art of politics is compromise."

For us in the United States of America, it's been that way from the beginning. The story of old Caesar Rodney, a Delaware delegate to the Congress ratifying the Declaration of Independence, illustrates it best.

That first Congress had decided any vote on independence would have to be unanimous.

South Carolina's, Pennsylvania's and New York's delegations would not go along and Delaware's two delegates present were split, one for, one against and one absent. The absent delegate, Caesar Rodney, was home in Dover with a canker sore on his face.

So the leaders of the Congress went to South Carolina's Rutledge, hung up over the slavery question, and asked him if he would support independence if they got all the other states to go along. He agreed—but only if he were the lone holdout.

Then they went to the Pennsylvania delegation, which was voting 4–3 against the Declaration. They talked two of the four into agreeing to stay home the next day, switching the vote to 3–2 for. New York indicated it would abstain.

Then they sent a rider to get old Caesar in Dover. They propped him up on a horse and he rode the ninety miles through a thunderstorm to get to Philadelphia. He walked in full of mud, cast his vote and we had a country.

And that's the way we do it today; ask members not to be the vote that hurts us, others just to stay home and others to come no matter what the cost.

And we have the greatest democracy known to man.

★

≣ 6 ≣

Doing the Right Thing
Is the Right Politics

One of my favorite congressmen, Lou Stokes of Cleveland, tells me he remembers where I made an impact on him. I had called in the Democrats of the House Budget Committee to get their support for a program of education, health and housing.

I told them of how, years ago, I had been able to persuade the chairman of the Appropriations Committee to put in some additional money for a drug to enable dwarfs to grow. I told them *The Wall Street Journal* even attacked the program as a waste of taxpayers' dollars. I told of how when I later visited a hospital at Baylor University, I saw these dwarfs that had actually grown by three inches. The point I was driving home was that as Democrats they had to be concerned about providing for social programs that really helped people.

I then told them they were worrying too much about their next election. I said to them I had been an elected official for more than fifty years and I have never looked down the road at my next election. I told them that if they would take care of the people, they wouldn't have to worry about the next election, the people would take care of them.

Lou said he never forgot my speech.

★

≡ 7 ≡

When Counting Votes,
Do It Yourself

The night before my election as majority leader, I had made all my calls to my colleagues and, feeling confident, went out to dinner with my two administrative assistants, Leo Diehl and Gary Hymel.

As we're going into Duke Zeibert's restaurant, where the pols still go, we saw a fellow who worked for Teddy Kennedy. Teddy was supposed to be reelected Senate whip the next day.

"How ya doing?" I said, knowing Ted had a race.

"Great, Tip," the fellow answered, "we've been making calls for Ted."

"Where's he?" I inquired.

"Down in Florida," the fellow said.

The next day, Bobby Byrd beat Ted for the whip's job.

What a lesson.

★

≡ 8 ≡

Compromise Is the Art of Politics

The hardest part of leadership is compromise. People often think when you compromise, you are compromising your morals or your principles. That's not what political compromise is. Political compromise is deferring your idea so a majority can be reached. That's what Congress does—gets 218 votes in the House and 51 in the Senate to pass a bill, or 60 votes to stop a filibuster in the Senate and solve a problem.

How do you get someone to go with you? Well, you appeal to their conscience, their patriotism, their party loyalty, their loyalty to you.

One thing—you never demand or threaten. You never want to be in the position of leading a member into defeat. You never ask them to commit political suicide.

One of my great assets was my experience as co-chairman of the Democratic Congressional Campaign Committee. I got to know all the congressional districts in America and how strong a member was in his or her own district. Then I knew how far I could ask them to go on a vote, how far to ask them to compromise.

One time I had to ask my pal, Joe Moakley, for a particularly tough vote in the Rules Committee. He said, "Jeez, Tip, that's a hard one."

"Hey, Josie," I said, "I don't need you on the easy ones."

He voted with me.

★

☰ 9 ☰

Be Loyal

Nothing is more valued in politics than loyalty, especially when it really counts, on a big vote.

Back in 1974, when we had the big freshman class of over sixty Democrats, we saw the first weakening of party loyalty. Most of that class was elected on its own, without the financial help of the Democratic Party. They went door-to-door and made it on their own. About a third of them had never been in public life before. They didn't know compromise and they didn't know loyalty. They were more educated and more sophisticated than any new members before them. They did their own thinking and didn't take leadership too well. We had a helluva time with them.

Of course, with experience, they came to realize that to govern, to get things done, they had to join into party voting.

Democracy can't work if it's every person for himself or herself.

★

≡ 10 ≡

Be Patient with Democracy

Our Founding Fathers knew what they were doing when they decided our form of government. The President proposes and the Congress disposes, all in due time.

The temptation, particularly for a new president, is to try to get it done too much too soon. Jimmy Carter made this mistake at the beginning of his presidency. He had too many balls in the air at the same time. He dropped a few and never fully recovered. Ronald Reagan was more focused on one thing, his economic plan, and succeeded. Bill Clinton had a lot of proposals going early, too.

But trust the system. The Constitution gave the representatives the right to deliberate and they just want to exercise it.

Other countries can't understand the role of the Congress. I must have met Deng Xiaoping of China a half-dozen times, and every time he would ask, "The President has to go to you for his money?"

Yes, and the President better not forget it.

The voters, the press and everybody ought to realize it. The system will work if you give it a chance.

Carl Albert, my predecessor as Speaker, once said that "our Founding Fathers didn't devise the most efficient form of government, only the freest."

★

No. 5
Using Clout

1

Once You Get Power Don't Be Afraid to Use It, No Matter How Big Your Opponent

It happened that I took on President Lyndon Johnson.

During Johnson's years in the White House, I had a couple of memorable encounters with the President. At one point, Robert McNamara, the secretary of defense, came to Boston and wanted to close the Boston Navy Yard in Charlestown. McNamara hoped to shut down unneeded military bases, and in the case of the Navy Yard he complained about everything—the quality of the work, the morale, and the cost overruns.

For my district, closing down the Navy Yard would have been an economic disaster. Besides, it was an excellent yard for shipbuilding, and was right on the sea-lanes to Europe. It was also the oldest shipyard in the Navy.

To get the President's attention, I walked out of a meeting of the Rules Committee just before a vote on a bill to reduce federal regulation of rail rates for perishable commodities—a bill the administration cared about. A few days later, Johnson called in the Democratic members of the Rules Committee for one of his periodic meetings.

As we were leaving, he took me aside. "Christ," he said, "we had the chance to get the transportation bill out, and you left! What's going on?"

"Mr. President," I said, "I'm spending a lot of my time trying to save the Boston Navy Yard."

"What do you mean?"

"McNamara keeps threatening to close it."

"Don't you worry about that," said the President. "That Navy Yard will be around as long as I'm in the White House."

And he kept his word.

★

≣ 2 ≣

"Pork" Pays for Itself— Eventually

You will read a lot about "pork barrel" projects being a waste of money. I don't believe it. A good definition of a "pork" project is one that's not in your area. These projects have to be economically justified or they don't get funded. Most are good investments, and I'll tell you about one.

Late in the seventies, representatives of Raytheon, the largest employer in my congressional district, came down to Washington to tell me the Army was threatening to cancel their contract to build the Patriot missile. The Army was claiming that tests on the missile were not showing a fast enough success rate. Raytheon claimed that every trial they conducted produced more knowledge and that they were able to make improvements. They were up to a 55 percent success rate.

I set up a meeting of the Massachusetts delegation with Joe Addabbo, the congressman who was head of defense appropriations, and had him watch a movie the Raytheon people had made. We were able to convince Joe that with additional trials Raytheon could ultimately achieve a 90 percent success rate. Of course, I was primarily interested in keeping those 8,000 people working at Raytheon.

Joe finally put money in the bill for the Patriot, and look at what happened almost fifteen years later. That great weapon saved lives in the Gulf War and is one of the technical marvels of today's military.

★

3

How to Package a Deal

Congressman Charlie Wilson of Texas, a guy who loves to play the rogue, was my victim on this one.

The Speaker has to nominate the Ethics Committee, and a difficult job it is. No member relishes having to judge his or her peers along the line.

Once, when I was announcing the members of the committee, I noticed Charlie making some wisecrack to Congressman Mo Udall of Arizona. He had Mo laughing and I had to find out what he was saying.

Mo came up to the rostrum and told me Charlie was critical of my choices for the committee, pointing out that my selections were all straight-laced, do-gooder-type members. He had opined that none of my choices was partial to strong drink or the opposite sex. (Charlie used more colorful language for these words.)

"Our caucus is not represented," Charlie had told Mo. "What about the principle of one man, one vote?"

The next time I had to appoint a member to the

committee, I remembered Charlie's observation. I also remembered he had been pestering me to get the congressional appointment to the board of the Kennedy Center. He always claimed I wouldn't appoint him to such a prestigious cultural institution because he was too much of a redneck. It wasn't true, of course. Other members who had jurisdiction over the center had a more justifiable claim on the appointment, but that was just Charlie's way of talking to get my attention. Now there was a vacancy opening up.

Well, I went to Charlie and asked him to take the Ethics spot. "No, Tip, you don't want me on that committee," he said. "I'm too much of an outlaw. I ain't your man."

"Do you want that appointment to the Kennedy Center?" I asked. "It's a package deal."

He took it.

★

≣ 4 ≣

In Politics, Sometimes You're Going to Disappoint Even Your Best Friends

I'll let Senator Tom Harkin of Iowa, who ran for President in 1992, tell this one on me:

"During my first term in Congress, when Tip was majority leader, a labor vote came up that I just couldn't support. I usually stand strong with labor. But I represented a tough rural district with very little labor, and this was one vote I just didn't agree with, and didn't think I could sell back home.

"Labor leaned on me really hard—they knew I had a tough race coming up, and they hinted that they might not support me if I didn't go along. They were really giving me a hard time.

"Well, I went in to see Tip and told him the situation. He brought the labor leaders in to see him, and said, 'I understand you boys are leaning on Congressman Harkin pretty hard for this vote. You know, he's the first Democrat since the Depression to represent his district, and this is a tough vote for him.'

"Then he said, 'You know, I've been in Congress now for over twenty years. And in all that time, I've disagreed with labor just twice. Can you believe it? In all that time—labor's only been wrong two times.'

"Well, that was a real icebreaker. The whole room busted up laughing, the tension was gone, and a few minutes later, the situation was resolved.

"I learned an important political lesson that day: In politics, sometimes you're going to disappoint even your best friends . . . but there's always tomorrow."

★

≣ 5 ≣

Remember Your Friends, and Who Their Enemies Are, Too

My pal Ted Stevens, the fine senator from Alaska, reminded me of something I did for him, and although I didn't have any particular political principle in mind at the time, I suppose there's one in there somewhere.

Ted for years had been trying to pass a bill to turn over the federally owned Alaskan Railroad to the state.

In the postelection session of 1982, a committee chairman in the Senate had held up the bill until the last minutes of the final day, then suddenly let it go, figuring there was no time to get it done in the House. The bill was called up in the Senate and passed. Stevens grabbed the bill, sprinted to the House chamber and ran up to the rostrum and handed it to me, explaining the predicament the chairman had put him in.

I called over Jim Wright, the majority leader, who I knew was angry with that same chairman for holding up a bill of his, and I said, "Jim, let's show the Senate how fast we can pass a bill." I mentioned the old chairman's name. Jim jumped at the chance. We passed the bill and today the railroad is on its feet and a great tourist attraction.

And we helped a friend and showed up his enemy.

★

≡ 6 ≡

You Don't Succeed by Climbing on the Backs of Your Colleagues

When I was selecting members to go on the Ethics Committee one year, the father of a newly elected member flew to Washington to ask me to name his son to the committee.

"If he can get on the Ethics Committee, he can become President of the United States," the father said.

I thought about the implications of that statement and ran a line through his name on my list of potential members.

★

7

If You've Got Power, Use It.
Your Friends Will Understand

Congressman Jack Murtha of Pennsylvania, one of my favorites, likes to tell people that everyone thinks I'm such a lovable guy, but that I can be tough when I have to be. "He's no pushover," Murtha says.

Jack's favorite story about me is the time I asked him to put $10 million in the Interior Department Appropriations bill for Tufts University, in my district.

Murtha ran into a problem: The chairman of the committee, Sid Yates, wanted to speak to me about the request. So I went to Sid and explained the grant. He said no.

Murtha rolled the chairman anyway, getting a majority of votes from my friends on the Republican side. In fact, Sid was the only one who voted against it. He even put restrictive language in the bill saying Tufts had to compete with other colleges for the grant.

Despite my opposition, the competitive process language stayed in the bill all the way to the conference with the Senate. My friend Eddie Boland was supporting it as a member of the conference committee and

I was scheduled to fly up to Springfield, Massachusetts, with him to speak at a gathering of 2,500 of his
constituents. I decided it was time to make my position clear.

I called in Murtha and asked him if the restrictive
language was still in the bill. He said it was, so I called
in Eddie and asked Murtha the question again in front
of him. Then I told Eddie I wasn't feeling well and
might have to cancel the trip.

"All right," said Eddie. "I'll oppose the language."

It came off and I took off for Springfield. And
Eddie understood. So did Murtha.

★

≡ 8 ≡

Be Ready with a Quip

My pal Eddie Boland was always ready with a snappy comeback. Once he appointed a young man to the Naval Academy and forgot about it until one night he learned they were going to kick the kid out of school. He called the superintendent to check on the circumstances and was told that the kid had gone over the fence, taken a car, was driving around with a girl, drunk, and had an accident.

"Furthermore," the superintendent added, he's at the bottom of his class!"

Eddie was his old unflappable self.

"Well, Admiral," he said, "somebody's got to be last!"

The admiral cracked up. "I never heard that one," he said. "Okay, I'll give him another chance."

The kid went on to captain a ship.

★

≡ 9 ≡

Use Your Clout

When Ronald Reagan was President, Garrett Fitz-gerald, the *taoiseach,* or prime minister, of Ireland, asked me to help start a new international fund to help Ireland and Northern Ireland. Many other countries were for it and it seemed like a good idea.

I sat down with Reagan and told him about how these other countries were agreeable on this and how it was time for us to join in. The figure was $200 million over five years. Reagan agreed.

I went to Dante Fascell, the chairman of the House Foreign Affairs Committee, and he told me the State Department had just testified against the plan. I called the State Department and was told, "You and the President are both for it. With that kind of strength, you don't need the State Department."

I figured I was being set up, so I called Reagan. "The State Department doesn't think this is the way to go but you gave me your word on it," I said. "I'm going to take a five-minute special order on the floor of the House and tell the world how you broke your word."

He said, "Give me five minutes."

Five minutes later, he called back.

"Okay, we'll go along," he said. "We politicians don't break our word."

★

≡ 10 ≡

Don't Make Artificial Lists

When I was Speaker, people would always be coming to me asking me to make lists of legislation. These people, usually the young liberals or the press, wanted me to give them a "must list" of bills that had to pass or some kind of priority list of what we were going to try to reach in a session of the Congress.

All a list is good for is for the press to use against you down the road so they can measure how you failed.

It's much better to take legislation one at a time, pass it and go on to the next one.

The "lists" will take care of themselves.

★

11

You Can Teach Old Dogs New Tricks

The toughest job I had as Speaker was passing a new ethics code. It was the first item on my agenda when I took over and it was clear the times demanded we do something in this area. We were going to get a pay raise that year and it would just be smart to couple it with some new rules about limiting outside income. Now, I have always said no one ever got beat voting for a pay raise, but a little insurance at that time wouldn't hurt.

The other leaders and I had agreed on one thing: We had to pass a bill that would require us to fully disclose all our assets. Most members saw the necessity of this—but not everyone. As Speaker, I had to get the bill out of the Rules Committee. You never heard such excuses. One older member didn't want to have to disclose his wife's financial assets because he feared it would make her a prime target for kidnappers. Another's wife was moving in high society and didn't want her fancy friends to discover how little her husband was worth. Another member didn't want to reveal how much in honoraria she was making—more than her salary.

I listened to all, let them vent their spleens, then told them the facts of life. We had to have an ethics code. I was firm and they knew I was right. You can teach an old dog new tricks but it helps if the old dog wants to learn. They learned to live with the new ethics code.

Another "old dog—new tricks" story is one President Johnson used to tell about when Senator Bob Kerr of Oklahoma found out at the 1960 Democratic convention in Los Angeles that LBJ was considering running as Jack Kennedy's vice presidential running mate. Kerr marched over to LBJ's suite and protested, "Lyndon, I hope you're not thinking about running with that liberal Irish boy from Boston! If you are, I'm going to take my thirty-thirty rifle and shoot you right between the eyes."

Hearing all this, Sam Rayburn took Kerr into the adjoining room, put his arm around him and said, "Now, Bob, you have your own race for reelection and Jack Kennedy will be right at the top of your ballot. Wouldn't it be better to have a neighbor like Lyndon on the ticket?"

LBJ said Kerr marched back into the room and said to him, "Lyndon, if you *don't* take that vice presidential nomination, I'm going to take my thirty-thirty rifle and shoot you right between the eyes!"

★

≡ 12 ≡

How to Stay on Schedule

It's tough to stay on schedule in politics. You make a schedule, try to stick to it, but the human element interferes. You simply have to make time if someone is really in distress and takes a little longer explaining their problem. You have to keep reminding yourself that that problem is the biggest thing in that person's mind at the time.

But you can do certain things to control your time. Good staffers know when to interrupt you and politely tell you your next appointment is waiting.

One of our most time-consuming practices in the House is the joint meeting with the Senate where we hear from some visiting head of state. Most members of Congress simply don't attend and sometimes it is embarrassing. When I became Speaker, I said only our two immediate neighbors, Canada and Mexico, would get automatic approval. The others could appear only if the President wrote me a letter requesting the joint meeting. With almost two hundred countries in the world and most of their leaders coming to

Washington, there was a big potential for joint meetings. My system cut it down considerably. I was tough; no exceptions—except for Ireland, of course. We did have a fallback, however: The Foreign Affairs Committee would have a reception for the head of state and I would go over.

I helped a lot of members' schedules that way.

★

No. 6
Street-Corner Truths

≡ 1 ≡

Any Candidate Has to Be Truly Dedicated to Public Service

When young people come to me today and say, "I want to get into government," I'm a little bit skeptical.

First of all, it's "politics" they are talking about, but they don't want to call it that. Now, there's nothing wrong with "politics" and they should be proud to say it.

I ask them why they want to get into "politics" and they say, "It looks like a nice career," "I want to reform the system," or "It's prestigious."

Nice? Reform? Prestigious? They don't get it. You've got to have a deeper purpose to be a politician. I always ran on a platform of what we called then work and wages. It means jobs, good pay and stimulating the economy to produce them. You can add education and the environment. Those are real reasons to run.

I guess I learned this at my father's knee. He was superintendent of sewers of the City of Cambridge, but he was more than that. There was always a long line of people at our house as people sought jobs and help. He always helped them.

Then, through my later life and campaigns, I would run into people who would tell me, "Oh, are you the governor's son?" That's what they called him. "Your father got me a job at the gas company." Or "My kid was retarded and your father got him a job as a janitor at the Knights of Columbus Hall."

Those people never forgot the hard work my father did for them.

I tell youngsters aspiring to politics today that they have to want to help people—that's what it's all about.

★

≡ 2 ≡

In Politics, Your Word Is Everything— Keep It and Good Things Will Happen to You

This one concerns the first time I met Jack Kennedy, who was running for Congress in 1946.

Jack was everywhere during that campaign, and he must have approached me seven or eight different times along the line to ask me to be with him. Again and again I explained I was with his opponent, Mike Neville, in the fight. Mike was my pal, he had served in the legislature with me and he deserved my support.

"But I'm going to win," Jack said.

"Maybe you will," I told him, "but I'm with Mike Neville if I'm with him alone. And I'm going to make damn sure we carry North Cambridge."

I was right about North Cambridge, but unfortunately for Mike, Jack was right about the election. He won with 22,183 votes. Mike Neville finished a distant second with 11,341.

The day after the election, Jack called me. "Tip," he said, "I can't tell you the number of politicians who announced they were with Neville but were working sub rosa for me. I was a little disgusted with them, to be honest, because they had given Neville their word.

"I don't know how many times I came to see you to ask for your support, but you always said no, that you were Mike's friend, and that you would bust your ass for him. I was sure I could win you over, but I was wrong. Well, you're a man of your word, and I can see that *when you're with a friend you're with him all the way.* The next time I run for office, I want you on my side."

Jack and I worked together from then on.

★

☰ 3 ☰

When You Join a Political Party, You Wait Your Turn

How many times have I seen a member of Congress try to leapfrog over another and fail? They forgot that the best way to move ahead is to do the job they are in and wait until their turn comes.

To me, the epitome of that was the story of the successor to Congressman Al Sabath.

When Sabath died, they held a special election in Chicago to replace him. Jim Bowler, who succeeded him, was seventy-eight years old. When Bowler came in, Eddie Boland went over and introduced himself. "Mr. Bowler," he said, "let me ask you something. Why did you want to come to Congress at the age of seventy-eight?"

"I'll tell you," he said. "Forty-six years ago, when I was just a young fellow, I served on the city council with Al Sabath. When a seat opened up in Congress, we took a vote to see which one of us would run. I received ten votes, and so did Al. We must have gone through twenty ballots, but it was still tied. Finally, we decided to flip a coin. The man who won would go to

Congress, and the man who lost would take his place when he was done.

"Al Sabath won the toss. He came to Congress and stayed for forty-six years. I've been on the city council all that time, and now that Al's dead, I figured it was my turn."

★

≣ 4 ≣

A Politician's Word Is His Bond

And it doesn't make any difference what condition he's in when he makes the commitment.

I had to resort to this principle with my old pal Mike Kirwan. Mike was a real operator in the House, and was chairman of the Subcommittee on Public Works of the House Appropriations Committee. He had so much power! At one point, Mike cut $3 million from the Cape Cod National Seashore project, although he had promised me personally that he would leave it in. I called him on the telephone. "Mike, you knocked out three million for Cape Cod."

"You're damn right I did," he said. "It's a waste of money and we've got better things to do."

"Hold on, Mike. We were having dinner at Paul Young's and you gave me your word that you'd put that money back in."

"Well, you're a nice son of a bitch, taking advantage of me when I was half stewed. But if that's really what I said, I'll put it back in." And he did.

★

≡ 5 ≡

Try to Keep People's Names Straight

Politicians who can remember names are golden. Jim Farley, who was chairman of the Democratic Party under FDR, had the greatest reputation for this. He had been national exalted ruler of the Elks and when someone would shout a greeting at him, he would answer with "Hi, Brother Elk." The fellow would usually reply, "He remembered me!"

I had been out in Kansas City for an off-year Democratic convention and was eating breakfast with House Rules Committee chairman Joe Moakley, a member from Massachusetts. Warren Beatty was there too, and Joe invited him to join us.

Not being a moviegoer, I had never heard of Warren Beatty. At one point, I turned to him and said, "You know, Warren, you're handsome enough to be in the movies."

Later, when Beatty had left, Moakley said, "You've got to be kidding. Don't you know that was Warren Beatty?"

"Who's Warren Beatty?"

"You know, the movie star."

"You mean the animal trainer?"

"Come on, Tip, you're thinking of Clyde Beatty. That was thirty years ago."

★

6

Sometimes the Great Names Can Help You—Usually They Don't

I was in a fight with Michael LoPresti and I came up with a surefire way to take the Italian vote away from him, or so I thought.

Now all you youngsters think the greatest fighter in the world was Rocky. Well, he is, but not Rocky Balboa. It's Rocky Marciano of Brockton, Massachusetts. My brainstorm was to get Marciano to endorse me. I got his picture in the paper with me and thought I was a genius. But he wasn't from the congressional district and it didn't mean a thing. The Italians voted for LoPresti anyhow.

I have known Carl Yastrzemski, the great Boston Red Sox outfielder, for over thirty years. When I first met him, he was so shy he would eat in the kitchen at our favorite hangout, Jimmy's Harborside Restaurant. When I had a reelection fight in 1968—my first since 1954—Carl wanted to help me. By then he was a big star, having won the triple crown. So we brought him to the Watertown Mall. The place was mobbed. Unfortunately, the crowd of 3,000 was there for Yaz—not me. In fact, no one was even paying attention to me. They pushed me out of the way to get to him. We solved that one by the next stop. In between, I got him to sign a thousand of my REELECT O'NEILL cards, which we handed out. So I got some notice, too.

★

≡ 7 ≡

Never, Never Buck a Line

When they brought the painting of the Mona Lisa over from the Louvre to the National Gallery of Art, the director called the office and invited me and my office staff to see it.

"We reopen at six o'clock so come about five forty-five and we'll let all of you in," he said.

So we all piled into two cars and went down to the gallery, but when we arrived a line about a half mile long had already formed. We did like we were told and went to the door, but when everyone in the line saw what was happening a tremendous roar went up. They booed the bejesus out of us. I never heard so much racket in all my life.

I should have known better. The only thing worse would have been if it were in my congressional district.

Those nice folks at the gallery were just trying to accommodate my staff without inconveniencing anyone. But it was not received that way, and we know, in politics, perception is as important as reality.

That same perception exists for many of the practices in the Congress today. Some of the tools the congressmen have to serve their constituents are seen as "perks" and often criticized. But the constituents demand service and members of Congress need people and materials to provide the service.

★

≡ 8 ≡

A Good Tipper Be

I met Jim McCarthy, a famous Irish rugby player and golfer, and told him I was headed for Ireland and planned to play at Lahinch, the world famous golf course.

"You'll know if you can play or if the weather's too rough by looking at the goats as you drive up to the clubhouse," he said. "If the goats are out chewing the lawn, you will be able to play. If they're on the porch, wait twenty minutes and you'll be able to play. But if they've climbed on the tables to get out of the rain, forget it and come by my house on the second green for a snack."

He was right. The goats were on the tables, so no golf. We went over to the house for a beer and Irish salmon.

Well, I wasn't going to let the day go to waste completely, so I told our hosts I wanted to see the famous cliffs of Moher, the highest cliffs in Europe, which were nearby. When we got there, no one else would get off the bus because it was raining so hard. So I went on alone. I got soaked to the skin but I was well rewarded. Huge waves were crashing into the cliffs, which are 700 feet high. The fog was rising and falling, making a magnificent sight.

I got back on the bus and everybody was high and dry and being entertained by a local man playing a harmonica. When he saw me he said, "Well, if it isn't himself, the great man Tip O'Neill, I know you well."

As he was leaving, I reached for my wallet to tip him but the bus driver stopped me.

"Don't touch him, he's got scurvy," he said. "In fact, he lives in an old automobile down by the cliffs. I've already given him something so don't give him anything." I didn't and the old man got off the bus grumbling.

We went on and I forgot about the incident until one day back in the States when I got a letter from some Iowa schoolteacher whose students had been entertained by the same harmonica player after we left. According to the teacher, "the charming shepherd" had asked, "Do you know the big man, Tip O'Neill?" They said they had heard of me. "Well, he was through here and I played for him and he may be Tip by name but he's not Tip by nature. He gave me nothing."

I must have gotten twenty letters from people who had read the column about this "darling leprechaun" in the high school newspaper.

I should have given him a fiver.

Other well-known people have the same problem.

I ran into the professional golfer Roger Maltby one

day and he told me about a favorite caddy of his. He told the caddy how excited he was, having been selected to play in the Bob Hope tournament with Hope, President Jerry Ford and me.

"You may be excited," the caddy said, "but any caddy will tell you something else about them. We call them Bob 'No Hope,' Jerry 'Can't Afford' and 'No Tip' O'Neill."

★

9

Term Limits Are Baloney.
Stick with the Old Oaks in a Storm

.

The United States has faced some tremendous crises in its history. The President and the Congress have faced them and solved them every time. But they have done it with experienced people, not rookies.

In my fifty years in politics, I have seen some real humdingers. First there was the Great Depression, with 55 percent living in poverty, 25 percent unemployed, only 8 percent with a pension plan and 3 percent with health insurance. When you reached fourteen, you got a work permit. Only 3 percent went to college.

Thanks to the President and the Congress and the will of the people, we got out of all that. The two greatest bills we ever passed were Social Security and the GI Bill.

I remember World War II. President Roosevelt's valet, Harry Fields, told us years later how bad things were after Pearl Harbor. Right after that sneak attack, Harry, who worked in the White House twenty-five years, was carrying the President to bed as he usually did, and FDR told him, "This looks bad. If the Japanese decide to invade, we can't stop them until they get to Detroit." But the President, the Congress and the American people rallied and stopped the Japanese and Hitler.

Then there was Sputnik. When the Russians put that ball in space, JFK stepped forward, promising to put a man on the moon in ten years. And we did it.

We didn't respond to all these crises with young fledglings. When the storm blows, the new saplings blow away. It's the sturdy old oaks that ride it out.

It's the same with political life. You have got to have the men and women with experience when the nation needs courage and stability. Put in term limits and you rob the nation of its best people in a time of need.

Trust the voters to regenerate the political institution when it needs change.

But don't put an artificial limit on quality. That's a big mistake.

★

≡ 10 ≡

Don't Forget to Use the Leftovers

My favorite mythical character is Uncle Dinny and I have a repertoire of his stories that I have told over the years.

It seems Uncle Dinny was at Mass one Sunday, sitting in the front row as usual, and the old monsignor was preaching on the Miracle of the Loaves and the Fishes.

"And the Lord took five thousand loaves of bread and two thousand fishes and he fed the five thousand," he boomed.

Well, Uncle Din wasn't going to let that go by, so on the way out he greeted the old monsignor at the door and told him he had gotten the numbers wrong.

The next Sunday, Din was on the front row and the old monsignor announced that he had made an error the previous Sunday. The Lord, of course, had taken five loaves and two fishes and fed the 5,000.

"Do you think you could do that, Din?" he asked from the pulpit.

"Yes," shot back Uncle Dinny.

"And how would you do it?" the old priest asked.

"I give 'em what was left over from last week," he said.

★

≡ 11 ≡

Fame Is Fleeting

I got on this airplane to fly to a book show in Akron, Ohio, and I thought I was in first class in seat 1A. The flight attendant informed me there was no first class and I was in 18A.

So I made my way to the back and sat down next to a young lady. "I heard they are holding the plane for some important person," she said. "Do you know who it is?"

"No," I said.

"What do you do?" she continued.

"I'm a book salesman," I answered.

About that time the man across the aisle recognized me and introduced himself. He said he had read a piece about me in *Cape Cod Life* and had carried the magazine in his briefcase hoping to run into me one day and get it autographed. I gladly signed the magazine.

Meanwhile, the young lady is observing all this and she finally blurts out, "I know who you are!"

"Who?" I said.

"You're—you're—you're the man in the American Express ad."

Another time, immediately after the Clinton inauguration, I went to a party in the Speaker's office run by one of my former employees, Barbara Sutton.

My granddaughter Michaela was with me and she got all excited. Michael Bolton had come in. She went over and got his autograph and he asked her, "Who's the old white-haired man over there signing autographs?" pointing to me.

"That's my grandfather, the former Speaker of the House," Michaela said proudly.

"Never heard of him," said Bolton.

I told Michaela I had never heard of Bolton either.

Another time I drove myself in Millie's car to speak at the Pan American Union. My staff had told me there would be a place reserved for me to park. I pulled into a spot marked RESERVED FOR THE SPEAKER.

The security guard, an elderly black man, came over and knocked on the window. "Get that car out of here," he hollered. "This space is reserved for the Speaker."

I got out of the car and said, "I *am* the Speaker."

He looked at me, did a double take, and said, "Mr. Rayburn, I didn't recognize you!"

This story has new life in the next generation with Speaker Tom Foley. Tom says when he was in New

Orleans at the New Orleans Athletic Club, one of the oldest health clubs in America, he had his usual workout and an attendant brought him a towel.

"I certainly enjoyed the workout and thank you for your help," said Tom.

The attendant, who Tom says must have been one of the original employees, replied, "You're welcome, and you come back any time you want, Mr. O'Neill."

Another time, after I had been out of the speakership about six years, I went to the House Credit Union to cash a check. I stood in line with about a dozen others, minding my own business. When I finally got to the window, I presented my check and the young man looked at it, and then asked if I had any I.D. with a picture on it. I told him I didn't and he went and got the manager. He had never heard of me either! Everybody roared.

Once I went over to the House Democratic Club for lunch and I found myself in the "O'Neill Room," very kindly dedicated in my honor. I was even standing under a portrait of my Irish self. The maitre d' looked up and said, "Do you have a reservation?"

How quickly they forget.

When I first arrived in the Congress of the United States, it was traditional on the first Wednesday of December for us to all go over to draw our office suites.

I walked into my new office and there was a portrait on the wall of former Speaker Champ Clark, I don't know why. Now, Champ Clark was the last man who got a majority of the vote of the Democratic delegates for the nomination for the President of the United States but who lost anyhow. In those days you needed a two-thirds vote of the delegates to the Democratic National Convention. Clark got a majority, but William Jennings Bryan revealed Clark had made a deal with Tammany Hall, the New York City machine, and he lost the nomination to Woodrow Wilson.

Back to Clark's portrait. I decided I wanted to put up pictures of my own district, so I called the Capitol architect and asked him to come get the portrait. He said he couldn't, he had no room to store it. So I went to Congressman Clarence Cannon, who was from Missouri like Clark, and asked him to take it. He was delighted.

Two years later, Cannon told me the story of what happened. It seems he gave it to Jefferson City High School in Missouri. They had a big dedication but after a while Cannon had second thoughts. He couldn't give away public property, and it was clearly property of the U.S. government or the artist. He did some checking. Turned out the artist was the loser in a competition for a portrait to hang in the Speaker's lobby in the Capitol. The artist was still alive, ninety-three, living in New Jersey. When Cannon asked him if it was okay to give it to Jefferson City High, he said no way, it belongs in the House of Representatives.

So back it came to my office.

Finally, one day I told the story to my old pal Congressman William Jennings Bryan Dorn of South Carolina and he said he'd take it. That's the last I saw of it.

Oh, fame.

★

≡ 12 ≡

Play the Numbers to Your Advantage

When journalists and political scientists were critically assessing the first hundred days of Bill Clinton's presidency (which I think is a stupid exercise), he received Stan Musial, the St. Louis Cardinal baseball star.

"Just think," said the President, eyeing the press, "Stan Musial is one of the greatest hitters of all time and he only got a hit once every three times at bat."

He would like to be judged by the same standard.

Jack Kennedy was a master at this sort of thing too.

When he was being criticized for being too young and inexperienced seeking the presidency, he invoked a baseball hero too. He noted Ted Williams of the Boston Red Sox was retiring at forty-two. Kennedy was forty-three.

He observed, "It seems that at forty-two, Ted Williams was too old. It shows that perhaps experience isn't enough."

Billy Sutton, Kennedy's first secretary, once gave an

interview in which he said, "There were only two .400 hitters in history, Ted Williams and Jack Kennedy."

I was a little hurt so the next time I saw Billy I asked him, "What about me?"

"You're the manager," he said.

★

≡ 13 ≡

The Critics Will Always Be with Us

Silvio and Corinne Conte were Millie's and my closest friends. We traveled together, went out to eat together and played bridge every Friday night when we were in Washington. We had a lot of laughs.

No question about it—Sil the congressman from Pittsfield, Massachusetts, did more for our state than the Kennedys, McCormack, Eddie Boland, Joe Moakley or I did combined. He had a big ego, though, and would tell you he was the world's greatest fisherman. (His fishing buddy, Carl Yastrzemski of the Red Sox, said Sil "couldn't cast into a bathtub.") He would also claim to be a great hunter. (His hunting pal, Father Bill George of Georgetown, said he "couldn't hit the side of a barn.") Oh, yes, he played football for Boston College and they lost to Harvard.

But he was a great storyteller and this was his favorite: "When I returned to my district office, there were long and loud complaints that I was spending too much time in the district and should be in Washington. Then when I didn't come home for several weeks others said, 'Who does that guy think he is? We only see him during elections.'

"When I came home shortly after being sworn in, driving my old car, they were upset because it looked like something farmers use to haul trash. But, by gosh, when I bought a new one they were sure the lobbyists had gotten to me already.

"The first time I came home wearing an old suit, I heard: 'Look at him. Just an old bum.' Yet, when I bought a new suit, I heard: 'He's gone high-hat with that Ivy League suit of his.'

"One Sunday I missed church because I was tied up with constituents, and some people said being down in Washington had made an atheist out of me. Several weeks later, when I was back home again and did get to church, they said, 'Why, that pious fraud, he's just trying to dig up votes!' "

★

14

Show Horses vs. Workhorses

In all my years in the Congress of the United States, the two best debaters I ever heard were Charlie Halleck of Indiana, the Republican leader, and John McCormack, my Speaker. Oh, how they went at each other, so talented and quick on their feet. If they had had C-SPAN, the whole country would have been amazed.

Halleck used to say the Senate had the show horses, the House had the workhorses.

Now the House has a rule limiting any member to five minutes of speech making. The Senate has unlimited debate.

Halleck used to say, "The average congressman can tell about all he knows on any given subject in five minutes. But over in the Senate they have unlimited debate and it takes them that long to prove that they know as much as we do."

★

15

Any Jackass Can Kick Over the Barn

I remember 1953 when I was sworn in as a congressman. The day before that the Democrats had their
caucus. It was a day I'll always recall. Sam Rayburn
had been Speaker the previous Congress, but now the
Republicans were in control of the Congress and Joe
Martin of Massachusetts would become Speaker.

As Speaker, Sam had called only one caucus a year.
He believed the caucus cut the power of the leadership and created dissatisfaction, disruption and ene-
mies within the party. Later the caucus was to become
potent, easy to call (any fifteen members of the party
can call a caucus) and automatically scheduled at
least once a month.

That day, Rayburn thanked the Democratic members for their continual faith in him and said he
wanted John McCormack as his No. 2 man. Contin-
uing, he talked about President Eisenhower. "A military leader," he said of Ike, "is accustomed to giving
orders and getting them carried out. He has no political, legislative or business experience. He's an Ameri-

can hero elected in a democratic election and treading on new fields. He'll need help. Remember that we are Americans first and Democrats second."

Then he made the remark that has lived in American history: "Remember, any jackass can kick over the barn, but it takes a carpenter to build one."

History shows how the Democratic leaders of the opposition party in the 84th Congress helped the President and met with him quite often. When those leaders gave their word, the party supported him.

★

= 16 =

Honorary Degrees Are Nice, but Don't Let Them Go to Your Head

During my lifetime I have gotten thirty-three honorary degrees and made thirty-one commencement speeches. Usually you are picked by the class, the president of the university, or the board of trustees. They ask their local congressman to ask me. It's hard to say no, but it is a day out of your life, and to be perfectly truthful, it doesn't mean that much to me.

One time Father Tim Healey, the outstanding president of Georgetown University, asked me to give the speech there. I had a golf date but I said I would do it.

Two days before the graduation he called me and said, "Mother Teresa is in town and would you let her give the commencement address? Could you give the speech to the law school?"

I told him, "Father, of course I'll yield to Mother Teresa, an inspirational lady."

But instead of taking the consolation prize, I declined and happily rescheduled my golf date.

★

≡ 17 ≡

The Right Joke—to the Right Crowd

An Irishman went into the Old Yankee Bank to get a loan to buy a house that was for sale for $2,000.

The old Yankee banker looked up the record of the Irishman's bank account, then he looked over the application for the loan, then he addressed the applicant. "Supplicant" was more like it.

"I have a standard test. I have one glass eye and one real eye. I'll give you the loan if you can tell me which is my glass eye and which is my real eye," he said.

The Irishman studied each of the banker's eyes carefully.

"The glass eye is the left eye," he finally pronounced.

"You're correct," said the banker, "but how could you tell?"

"It was easy," said the Irishman. "The left eye had the warmth in it."

I've told that at a hundred bankers' conventions and they love it every time.

★

≡ 18 ≡

Get the Bad News Too

Whenever I'd see my staff for the first time that day, I'd ask, "What's new?" And I meant it—give me the good news and the bad news.

If your staff thinks you can't take the bad news, for fear you will behead the messenger, something is wrong with you. You are paying them to provide you with information. They shouldn't fear you.

I wanted the bad news because then I could do something about it, and fast.

Another good piece of advice is, ask your staff periodically, "Am I the same person you went to work for?"

★

Today's Adversary May Be Tomorrow's Ally

Lindy Boggs, a great congresswoman and a lovely person, used to say, "Always say 'please' and always say 'thank you.' "

That's why no one could ever say no to Lindy.

I had my own story about this one. I ran for the Massachusetts legislature six times and a total of 118 persons ran against me. The day after every election, I'd call my opponents, thank them and ask them for their support in the general election. When I ran for Congress in 1952, all 118 signed an ad for me.

Always regard and respect your opponents.

★

≡ 20 ≡

Be Distinctive

When Father Robert Drinan came to Congress, he wanted to know if he should wear his black suit and Roman collar on the House floor. Sure, I said, otherwise you'll be like everybody else. He did and he sure wasn't.

Then there's that story about Sam Rayburn, who dealt with just the "old bulls" of the House. One day he acknowledged a freshman member, Danny Inouye of Hawaii, who had lost an arm in World War II. Rayburn told him that after the Speaker, the new freshman was the best-known member.

"Me?" said Danny.

"Of course, you," said Rayburn. "Well, just think about it, son. How many one-armed Japanese do you think we have in the Congress of the United States?"

★

≡ 21 ≡

There Can Be Change for the Better

When I was reelected to Congress in 1954, the Democrats had recaptured the Congress and Sam Rayburn was to return to the speakership after having been minority leader. But Rayburn was reluctant to run again for Speaker. In a leadership meeting with his pals, Sam talked about the ability, friendship and loyalty of his dear friend and No. 2 man, John McCormack. The news of Rayburn leaving was floated, a trial balloon went up and it was quickly shot down. McCormack was a Catholic and it was doubted that any Catholic could be elected Speaker of the House. So Rayburn was elected. Remember, this was 1954. Jack Kennedy would be elected President before the doors of the House would be opened to a Catholic as its Speaker. McCormack finally was elected Speaker after the death of Rayburn, but only after the election of Jack

Kennedy had overcome the question of religious bigotry in this country. It's hard to believe this was such a short time ago. Every minority can take some hope from that change for the better.

★

22

Labels Can Be Deceiving

I was always a great fight fan. I remember meeting the great Boston boxer Honeyboy Finegan, a legend in our time, who went on to become a successful businessman and was a real role model to us Irish youngsters. He told me he had fought Goldie (Goldstein) Ahern, a tough little Jewish welterweight.

In the twenties the Irish were the great fighters and the Jews took Irish names to capitalize on their success, like Goldie Ahern.

Anyway, Goldie was fighting Billy Murphy in Lynn, Massachusetts, at the outdoor park that was the first lighted ballpark ever. I'd been there many times in the late twenties and thirties.

If Murphy could get by Goldie, he had a shot at the welterweight championship of the world.

But that wasn't happening. Goldie was handling him easily in the early rounds, but knowing Murphy was a local boy from Lynn, he decided to carry him awhile longer. In the sixth round, a fan screamed to

Murphy, "Hit him in the belly, Murph. Hit him in the belly. Jews can't take it in the belly!"

Instead, Goldie starts pummeling Murphy in the belly and Murphy finally yells, "Hey, Goldie, take it easy, I'm Jewish too!"

I told this story to a group that included Ab Mikva, the former congressman who's now a federal judge (who should be on the Supreme Court), and Ab said, "Tip, even the ACLU would like that one."

★

No. 7
What Every
Politician
Needs to
Know

≡ 1 ≡

Treat Everyone Alike—Nice

Remembering that is what made my career. Mayor James Michael Curley, the legendary pol of Boston, taught me this early. "Over the years," he said "hundreds and hundreds of people will come to your office and ask you for favors. Some of these favors may be great, and some of them may be small. Some may be important, and some may be trivial. Some will be easy, some will be difficult.

"But always remember, for the person who comes to you, that favor is the most important thing in the world. If he could take care of it himself, he wouldn't be coming to see you. So treat them all alike and try to help everybody—no matter how big or how small the problem is."

Curley told me something else and I've never forgotten that one either. He said, "Son, it's nice to be important. But remember—it's more important to be nice."

A good example of this happened to me early in 1966 when I was sitting alone in my congressional office in Boston waiting to go to an official banquet. It was about seven P.M. and the door was open.

A fellow walked in and introduced himself as George Shapiro. "What's on your mind?" I said. He told me that he was from Brookline in my district. It seems his son had married a Turkish woman whose parents wanted to remain in the United States.

I said I would help by filing a bill to stop them from being sent back. In those days that's all it took. You can't do that anymore.

Anyway, the bill finally passed, and the fellow was oh so grateful. He said I had restored his faith in the government, that he thought he might have had to buy their way in.

In my next election he insisted on giving me a party. And what a party it was; at his estate, with a tent and an orchestra. A thousand of his friends came. It really was a grand affair, but, to be perfectly truthful, I didn't need it. Brookline was always one of my strongest neighborhoods. I usually carried it 7,000 to 400. But it was nice to be remembered.

More recently, I got a similar reward.

On my eightieth birthday my family and friends threw a big party for me in Washington and one of the biggest surprises was a beautiful video message from President Clinton and Vice President Gore, whom I knew from when he was in the House.

It turned out the video was the idea of Jim Desmond, a great Irishman and pal of mine, and a fellow named Tom Hoog, the head of the Hill and Knowlton office in Washington, who knows the President.

I called Tom to thank him and he said, "Well, Mr. Speaker, it's payback time. You don't remember this, but once I was sitting in the next box to you at a Red Sox game and the players came over to tell you hello. My kids asked you to get their autographs and you got them from Carl Yastrzemski, Carlton Fisk, Freddie Lynn and Dwight Evans. One future Hall of Famer and three all-time greats, and the kids still have the balls. It was one of the biggest moments in their lives. So thank *you*."

★

2

How to Lobby Your Congressman Effectively

There was nothing more frustrating to me than to have some businessman or constituent come in and launch into a diatribe about "H.R. 3516" or "H. Res. 402," repeating that bill number until I was dizzy.

Now, I know that piece of legislation was the most important thing on that person's mind, but there are 45,000 bills introduced every year and "H.R. 3516" or "H. Res. 402" meant nothing to me.

If you are going to visit your congressman to ask for help, follow some simple steps to be effective. First, write and request an appointment and tell him or her what you want to talk about. Cite the legislation you are interested in by number and content. Then by the time you arrive, the member of Congress will have had his staff check on the bill, where it is in the legislative process and its chances of passage into law.

Make sure you are prepared on your subject and know both sides of your argument. The congressman will probably ask you what problems he might encounter if he helps you. Help him help you.

Also, have your views on a piece of paper you leave behind with him. Then he and his staff can follow up for you and notify you when the vote occurs.

As for paid lobbyists, every member knows they are representing particular constituencies. They are valuable because they have information that can help you. They know their subject and can tell you who is going to be helped and who is going to be hurt by a particular bill. The word *lobbyist* has a negative connotation but in most cases such a reputation is undeserved.

I have many good friends who are lobbyists and they are good people. My favorite was Evie Dubrow, the lobbyist for the International Ladies' Garment Workers Union. Evie never asked for a raise because her salary came from the sweat of the brow of her employees, the garment workers. I love her for that. She could come into my office without knocking and she is the only person the doorkeepers let sit in their chairs at the entrance to the House chamber.

★

☰ 3 ☰

Keep Your Perspective

Being a politician is a tough job. If you do it right, it means long hours, constant interruptions, tension-filled debates, stressful decisions and surrendering your privacy.

You have got to know how to step away from it all periodically to regenerate yourself.

I have always found golf to be a great relaxer. I can get out there on the course and forget about all the problems we have to face today. I can also enjoy a good game of cards and occasionally a drink to break the tension. A good laugh with a good friend does it too.

A good lesson in keeping your perspective is: Take your job seriously but don't take yourself seriously.

★

≡ 4 ≡

Make a Connection

For a politician to be successful, he or she is going to have to meet a lot of people. Connecting with them on an individual basis is crucial, I don't care how many TV sound bites they get.

You have to find that common ground you have with each person you meet, be it through hometown, ethnic group, sport or anything else.

There's a line to everybody and you have to find it. It makes people feel at home and they love you for establishing the link.

★

≡ 5 ≡

Knowing When to Say Yes and When to Say No

When I was a leader in the Congress of the United States, members were always coming to me with ideas and advice. Some were worthwhile and helpful. Most of them weren't. But you just couldn't reject them out of hand.

I found if I put my arm around the member and promised to take a good look at it, it went a long way. Someone said if O'Neill gave you a bear hug going in, it was okay, but if you got a bear hug going out, you'd lost.

The best way to handle this is to try to be prepared. Have an intelligence network that tells you about problems before they occur. Have a good staff to spot the crackpots. My administrative assistant, Leo Diehl, was called my goaltender, the way he kept the pests out.

No politician likes to say no. A lot of times you can get your staff to do it. Or you can promise to study the question. Time solves a lot of problems.

★

6

Get Yourself a Good Accountant

Especially these days when everything is reportable and the report is available to the press and the public.

The best thing is to get a personal friend, one who is qualified, to keep the books. You can't go wrong if you keep good records.

One of my political accounts had just $164 in it and one of the secretaries who had to file reports on it asked me if we could close it out by giving it to her congressman. I said okay, and I'll bet that congressman is wondering today how he got such an odd contribution. He doesn't know whether it should have been $150 or $200.

In the old days there weren't as many rules as there are now and the press wasn't as critical.

The ethics of politics has changed. Politicians who don't realize that are making trouble for themselves if they don't cross every *t* and dot every *i*.

★

≡ 7 ≡

It's Easier to Run for Office Than to Run the Office

In a campaign, the candidate raises expectations and convinces the voters he or she can walk on water. That's what the whole effort is about.

Then comes the time to deliver.

It used to be that the President had a honeymoon period where the people and the Congress gave him the benefit of the doubt and went along with his ideas. Not anymore. The opposition party pounces right away, the press tackles him without restraint or courtesy.

No one learned this quicker than did President Clinton. His campaign created expectations. A few changes of position caused him tremendous damage. He won the big votes, but the Republicans and the press hammered him with the small things.

Politicians have to realize, I always say, that just like at the track, the horse that runs fast at the beginning often doesn't run long.

★

≡ 8 ≡

Never Say Something You Don't Want to See on the Front Page of the Local Paper

Politicians have to understand the role of the press. Reporters are there to get a story. My administrative assistant, Leo Diehl, likened them to a political candidate, campaigning for a story.

The trick is to not take their questions personally. If they ask a mean one, pause and count to three before answering. And remember, you don't have to be responsive to every question. It's a hard thing to do. When someone wrote a mean or unfair thing about me, they went on my list. You know the one.

But I also know you shouldn't get into a fight with someone who buys their ink by the barrel or their film by the case.

The best way to handle them is to be straightforward with them. I always tried to be helpful. As a leader, I felt we had an obligation to keep the public informed and the press was the way to get the information out. That's the bedrock of our open democracy.

As Speaker, I had a fifteen-minute press conference

every day. I rather enjoyed the banter and the reporters soon learned I had no personal agenda or devious plans. And when I made a mistake like confusing "billions" with "millions" they wouldn't report it.

One time a particularly obnoxious reporter did a mean piece on me and demanded a follow-up interview. I called a press conference with all the press corps on Capitol Hill and he showed up with a stenographer to try to nail me. In front of all his colleagues, he ended up looking stupid.

Not all reporters are alike. Some are just doing their job. Others are out to get you. Don't help them make the story. Keep your cool.

My old pal Jimmie Burke used to say, "Don't write it if you can talk, don't talk if you can wink, and don't wink if you can nod."

And take care of your local press first. They'll get the story straight. They usually want to help.

★

9

Stick with the Two-Party System

The beauty of American democracy is the two-party system. Just look at the other democracies of the world with all of their parties. The only way their governments work is through coalitions. But coalitions break up periodically and governments fall. Chaos.

Our two parties pit one philosophy against the other. One wins and one loses and we have stability. Sure, we have threats of a third party movement all the time. They sometimes provide a good idea, like the Progressive Movement and the Populists, but one of the two major parties will incorporate those ideas in the next election and we continue with the two-party system.

We have diversity within our parties. The Democrats are really about five parties in any other country, moving across the liberal to conservative spectrum. The Republicans are a lot more homogeneous.

I remember when the Democrats could all but ignore the South because we could attract thirty-five moderate Republicans. Now the Southern Democrats are necessary for Democratic victories. I believe Ronald Reagan unified the Republican Party.

The pendulum swings but the two-party system has stood the test of time.

★

≡ 10 ≡

Learn to Disagree Without Being Disagreeable

Everyone knows that President Reagan and I had a lot of disagreements. Some of our arguments got pretty heated.

One time we were going at it pretty good at a White House leadership breakfast and Al Simpson, the Republican whip, stopped us.

"You two Irishmen are confusing us," he said. "You give out with all that Irish charm, telling stories and swapping jokes, then you get in here and start all this fighting. I can't keep up."

Of course, the argument stopped. He was right. You have to learn to disagree without being disagreeable.

★

≡ 11 ≡

Know When to Quit

Most people don't leave public life too happy. Sometimes the voters have to tell them. Sometimes their family and friends have to tell them and they don't like it.

One of the things I did right was get out when I did. I left before I got pushed.

I remember reading that Senator William Fulbright said he was "frustrated" with Congress. This from a man who founded the Fulbright Scholars Program and did such a great job pursuing the Vietnam War issue.

I think if you get frustrated over a long period of time or find yourself getting cynical or find yourself hiding from your voters or your colleagues, it's time to get out.

It's one of the things politicians do least well.

The story of how Rocky Marciano quit the ring had a profound effect on me, probably because I was there.

Marciano was an outstanding person. He was still

champ when my classmate and pal Monsignor John "Speed" Carroll got him to attend a CYO event at which I was speaking. Cardinal Richard Cushing, the celebrant, told Rocky at the communion rail that he wanted to see him afterwards. Twenty minutes later, Rocky came out ashen-faced. I asked him what the cardinal wanted. "He told me how grateful I should be that God had given me so much strength and such a sense of decency. I had come through all those fights without getting my brains scrambled. He said he wanted me to pledge I'd never fight again. I gave him my word on the altar of God I would never fight again."

And Rocky told me he never would. And he never did.

★

▤ Tip's Political Checklist ▤

1. Vote your conscience, your country, your district, the leadership, in that order.
2. Never question the honesty or integrity of a colleague.
3. It's a round world—what goes around, comes around.
4. You can accomplish anything if you're willing to let someone else take the credit.
5. Never lose your idealism.
6. Lead by consent, not demand.
7. The bigger the crowd, the lower the vote.
8. Learn to say, "I don't know but I will find out."
9. K.I.S.S.—Keep it simple, stupid.
10. Don't stay mad—there's always tomorrow. Today's enemy is tomorrow's ally.
11. Never speak of yourself in the third person.

12. Tell the truth the first time and you don't have to remember what you said.

13. The horse that runs fast early fades in the stretch.

★

ACKNOWLEDGMENTS

It certainly was fun doing this book. Just recalling all the stories I heard and told in a lifetime of politics about all the characters in Boston and Washington was a pure pleasure for me. One of the advantages of age is that you can remember clearly things that happened forty and fifty years ago. You just can't remember where you put your glasses this morning.

I would like to acknowledge a few people responsible for help on this book. The idea was Jay Acton's, my agent. He thought there ought to be a record somewhere of all my stories and political principles. My publisher, Peter Osnos, and the editor Jonathan Karp both did their jobs well, diplomatically curbing my tendency towards what Peter calls "pontifical bloviation." We Irish do tend to go on a bit too long.

A special hug has to go to my wife, Millie, for enduring all the stories over a lifetime. Her I excuse from reading this book.

Then there are the people I quoted, and didn't quote. They include:

James Michael Curley; President Jack Kennedy; Speakers John McCormack, Sam Rayburn, Tom Foley and Carl Albert; State Senator John Parker; Presidents Harry Truman, Lyndon Johnson and Bill Clinton; and Thomas P. O'Neill, Sr., my father, a political leader.

Congressmen Silvio Conte, Eddie Boland, Joe Moakley, Jimmie Burke, Lou Stokes, Charlie Wilson, Jimmy Duncan, "Pete" Peterson, Michael Kirwan, Jack Murtha, Bill Hungate, Charlie Halleck, Charlie Weltner, Lindy Boggs and Jim Bowler.

Senators Alan Simpson, Ted Stevens, Tom Harkin, Ed Muskie and Danny Inouye.

Millie O'Neill, Kip O'Neill, Rosemary O'Neill, Jackie O'Neill, Leo Diehl, Danny Thomas, Evelyn Dubrow, Tom Hoog, Father John "Speed" Carroll, Rocky Marciano, Bishop Fulton Sheen, Carl Yastrzemski, Ted Williams, Roger Maltby, Bill Barnstead, Dorothy Kelley, Dick Furbush, Uncle Dinny, Sonny McDonough, Father Tim Healey, Ben Franklin, Pat Brown, Bob O'Hare, Tom Findley, Honeyboy Finegan, Peter Hart and Tom Buckley.

Barbara Montgomery and Kate Monahan did the typing, and did a good job, too.

★

About the Authors

THOMAS P. O'NEILL, JR., was a Massachusetts state representative and Speaker, a congressman, whip, majority leader and Speaker of the U.S. House of Representatives from 1977 to 1986. His first book, *Man of the House: The Life and Political Memoirs of Speaker Tip O'Neill*, was a bestseller.

GARY G. HYMEL worked as a reporter in New Orleans and as administrative assistant for Hale Boggs and Tip O'Neill in the U.S. House of Representatives' offices of majority whip, majority leader and Speaker. He is vice chairman of Hill and Knowlton Public Affairs Worldwide.

★